HOW
I PLAY
GOLF

HOW I PLAY GOLF

BY TIGER WOODS

WITH THE EDITORS OF
GOLF DIGEST

WARNER BOOKS

A Time Warner Company

Warner Books, Inc.
1271 Avenue of the Americas
New York, NY 10020

Visit our Web site at www.twbookmark.com

For information on Time Warner Trade Publishing's
online publishing program, visit www.ipublish.com

• • •

A Time Warner Company

Printed in the United States of America

First Printing: October 2001
10 9 8 7 6 5 4 3 2 1

• • •

Library of Congress Cataloging-in-Publication Data
Woods, Tiger.
How I play golf / Tiger Woods with the editors of *Golf Digest*.
p. cm.
ISBN 0-466-52931-1
1. Golf. I. Golf digest. II. Title.
GV965 . W743 2001
796.352'3—dc21   2001026495

• • •

Book Design: Judith Turziano
Cover Design: Flamur Tonuzi

• • •

PHOTO CREDITS
Cover photography by Jim Moriarty

All photography by *Golf Digest* staff photographers
Stephen Szurlej, Dom Furore and Jim Moriarty, unless otherwise noted.
Allsport, Endpaper, VII, 42, 208, 209, 210-211, 212-213, 261, 272-273, 274, 278, 282-283, 291;
Corbis/Jerry Tubby; Elizabeth Whiting and Associates, 284-285; Bob Ewell, 304-305;
Bill Fields, 77; Rusty Jarrett, 80, 234-235; Larry Lambrecht, 15 (*left*);
Gary Newkirk, I, 128-129, 142, 206, 226, 227, 244, 257, 267; Larry Petrillo, 276;
Kultida Woods, VIII, 4, 260; Illustrations by Ed Acuña, 28-29, 63, 70, 116, 135, 151, 240-241;
John Corbitt, 12-13, 22, 25, 27, 33, 46, 61, 69, 77, 87, 92, 119, 122, 145, 165,
174, 217, 222-223, 243, 246, 258-259, 265, 266, 286, 288-289

To Mom and Pop,

whose love and support

sustain me.

CONTENTS

PREFACE

When Tiger Woods signed an exclusive agreement to write instruction articles for *Golf Digest* in June 1997, there was elation on the part of the editors, and one concern: Was Tiger's knowledge of the golf swing broad and sophisticated enough to convey advice that would help the average golfer improve? Tiger was 21 years old, an age where most players "hit 'em and hunt 'em" without much regard to swing mechanics or strategy. There was no denying his talent as a player—he had won the Masters Tournament just two months previous—but our expectations of Tiger the author/teacher were modest to say the least.

Like the rest of the world, we underestimated Tiger. The first research session with him was a revelation. His grasp of the fundamentals was complete. His understanding of cause and effect in the full swing was astonishing and would grow even richer through time. What's more, his explanations were expansive, articulate and ordered perfectly. He quickly displayed a knack for phrasing his advice in a way that embraced the widest range of golfers possible.

The sum of what Tiger knows about golf is presented in this book. Happily for the reader, Tiger's knowledge has increased over time and extends well beyond his contributions to *Golf Digest*. Tiger's new commitments to physical conditioning, diet, sport psychology and insight into being a tougher competitor are presented here for the first time.

Despite Tiger's eagerness to assist the everyday golfer, the title of this book is *How I Play Golf.* Take note of the "I." Tiger insisted at the outset that he focus on what's right for *him*. Yet, you'll find his methods are sound and far-reaching. When Tiger discourses on the fine points of how he drives the ball 350 yards, you can take comfort knowing that the advice will assist you in your quest for more distance.

At age 25, Tiger has achieved an all-encompassing command of himself, his sport and the world that surrounds it. We hope you enjoy this insight on every facet of the game from the greatest player of his time.

—THE EDITORS OF *GOLF DIGEST*

What a ham: Tiger has been teaching us from the beginning.

FOREWORD

At the 2001 Masters I witnessed Tiger's complete metamorphosis that culminated in a record-setting run of four consecutive major championship victories. His historic accomplishment, inconceivable just two years before, was awesome to behold. Words cannot describe the pleasure and pride I felt when he came into my arms as he walked off the 18th green that Sunday afternoon, the sun sinking behind those huge pine trees. Four years earlier it was a similar scene after Tiger won his initial Masters during his first full year on tour. This time was different. This time I embraced a grown-up who had tried on the title of *best in the world* and found it a perfect fit. I said to him, "You pulled it off. Now you really are in the history books. I love you."

This journey began in the high chair in my garage in Cypress, Calif., where a six-month-old baby watched intently as his father hit balls into a net. Amazingly, he had an attention span of two hours. From the beginning, Tiger had a beautiful, fundamentally sound golf swing. There was just one problem: He was left-handed. It took him two weeks to discover that I was on the other side of the ball. In the middle of a swing, he stopped, walked around on the other side of the ball, changed to a right-handed grip and proceeded to hit the ball into the net perfectly swinging right-handed. I witnessed it and still can't believe it.

His swing developed as he grew older. When Tiger was a teenager it was long, loose and relatively flat. Then he went through a growth spurt and his instructor, John Anselmo, changed his swing plane to more upright to prevent him developing "hookitis" that characterized the early days of Hogan. This swing prevailed through junior and amateur golf. But I knew it had flaws that would have to be corrected. After being eliminated in match play at the 1993 U.S. Amateur at The Champions in Houston, Tiger was reviewed and evaluated by Butch Harmon. Tiger hit a few balls for Butch, who made a startling statement. "Tiger," he said, "Greg Norman had a great pair of hands, but you have the greatest hands I have ever seen." He immediately had Tiger's attention. He then told him, "I'll bet on the downswing, just before impact, you sense whether the club is opened or closed and you make an adjustment with your hands." Tiger said, "Yes, I do." Butch told him they would eliminate that problem by making Tiger's swing plane more consistent to permit the club to come into the hitting area square. Tiger would then be able to use his hands to work the ball. I moved to the edge of the range and watched them work. It was the beginning of a wonderful relationship.

All along, Tiger has been a keen student of the game, displaying tenacity, courage and heart. When he was 8, I told him that he had that extra gear that all great athletes display and that he could call upon it at any time. He knew what I was talking about because we had discussed this while watching players like Magic Johnson, Larry Bird and Kareem Abdul-Jabbar perform their best under pressure. Tiger demonstrated that same ability very early in his development. Setting records at every level of participation, he established a standard of excellence for aspiring golfers. At each level he had the added responsibility of being a minority. Watching him perform under difficult circumstances was inspiring.

Tiger has been a teacher his entire life. I know he has taught me things. The exhibitions he staged for inner-city youth as a teenager have evolved into orchestrated clinics under the auspices of the Tiger Woods Foundation. Just like Tiger, they are competitive in nature, in that each city must submit a proposal to obtain Tiger's services. At his insistence, these clinics are not just ball-striking exhibitions. They present a unique history of the game along with its rules and job opportunities. He is a living example of his family's credo of care and share. I hope this work of love will unlock the door to a wonderful game for those who share in his passion for it. Within its pages you will find wisdom, guidance, technical tips and pure instruction. Listen to Tiger's heart. It is speaking to you. I trust that you will get the message.

—EARL WOODS, *Autumn 2001*

ACKNOWLEDGMENTS

Many thanks to *Golf Digest*

and Warner Books for their collaborative effort

in making this project possible.

Also, grateful acknowledgments to my early teachers

Rudy Duran and John Anselmo, Jay Brunza,

Butch Harmon, who has been my friend and teacher since 1993,

Steve Williams, who has been at my side through many tough rounds

and great moments, writers Pete McDaniel and Guy Yocom,

photographers Dom Furore, Stephen Szurlej and Jim Moriarty,

Golf Digest managing editor Roger Schiffman

and designer Judy Turziano.

FIRST THINGS FIRST

❖ ❖ ❖

Golf is a never-ending journey.

Before we begin, we should

look at where we've been.

HOW TO START

YEARNING TO LEARN

I love golf as much for its frankness as for those rare occasions when it rewards a wink with a smile. It is pure, honest and immune to sweet talk. Neither can it be bum-rushed. You must court it slowly and patiently. Any other strategy will be met with a rebuff that for centuries has made grown men and women cry.

Golf does, however, show you moments of vulnerability. They are the reason we relish the courtship and the basis for our hope. It is that flicker of anticipation that draws us from the comfort of ambivalence to the certainty of rejection. Golf does not play favorites. Still we try.

I have been infatuated with the game since my pop first put a club in my hands when I was a toddler. I was an only child, and the club and ball became my playmates. That feeling of solitude and self-reliance enhanced the game's attraction for me and endures today. I suspect that is true of most people who have succumbed to the lure of the game. I recall from conversations with two of the greatest golfers of our time— Arnold Palmer and Jack Nicklaus—that the game had a similar appeal for them. Golf affords you supreme independence. The cliché about the game being you against the golf course is only partly true. Ultimately, it is you against yourself. It always comes down to how well you know yourself, your ability, your limitations and the confidence you have in your ability to execute under pressure that is mostly self-created. Ultimately, you must have the heart and head to play a shot and the courage to accept the consequences.

Golf is a great mirror, often revealing things about you that even you didn't know. It cannot be misled. Still we try.

Sometimes the game comes so easily you can hardly believe it. Every swing seems natural and unforced. Every shot comes off exactly as you envisioned it. That false sense of security is part of the seduction. Every golfer has experienced it. If we are honest with ourselves, we'll admit never quite reaching nirvana—that feeling of invincibility. We are constantly on edge. There is no comfort zone in golf. Nor is it a game of perfection. If it were, we'd all shoot 18 and look for a more challenging sport. I shot a 61—my lowest competitive round—in the third round of the Pac-10 Championships during my sophomore year at Stanford and bogeyed the par-4 14th hole. I actually hit the ball better

YOUNG AND (EAGER) RESTLESS

From the beginning I was taught the many facets of golf, that it was much more than just hitting the ball, finding it and hitting it again. It has been a constant learning process with experiences I wouldn't trade for anything. I learned how fundamentals, like never getting the club past parallel on the backswing, were essential for playing the game properly. I also discovered that early success helped boost my confidence and how that translated into a distinct advantage in competition. The trophies were nice, too, but meeting a legend like Sam Snead and getting his autograph were just as cool.

during the afternoon round and shot four strokes worse, including a bogey at 15. Only once do I recall feeling nearly in control of my game and that was when I shot a 13-under-par 59 at my home course in Orlando. Even then I parred both par 5s on the back nine with irons into the greens. The most we can ask of ourselves is to give it our best shot, knowing that sometimes we will fail. We are often defined by how we handle that failure.

The great Ben Hogan, a man not prone to exaggeration, claimed that in his best week of golf he only had four perfect shots. I have yet to get to that higher plane. I won 12 times around the world in 2000, including three majors, and I only remember hitting one shot I would call perfect—a 3-wood on No. 14 on the Old Course at St. Andrews in the third round of the British Open. From a tight lie I had to hit a little draw into a left-to-right wind and carry the ball about 260 yards to a green guarded by a couple of nasty pot bunkers. As with every shot I attempt, I visualized the ball's flight and how it should respond upon landing. Because it was a blind shot, I picked out a crane in the distance as my target. The ball never left that line and the shot turned out exactly as I had planned. Moments like that stay fresh in my mind, providing a positive image for future reference. Those images are critical when the game is on. They may even be the difference between success and failure.

Sometimes the game seems so difficult you

Reverence for those who helped shape this great game is a responsibility as well as an honor.

*I am a naturally
shy person and much
more comfortable on
the golf course than
perhaps anyplace else.
However, winning
makes press conferences
more enjoyable. Some-
times they're even fun.*

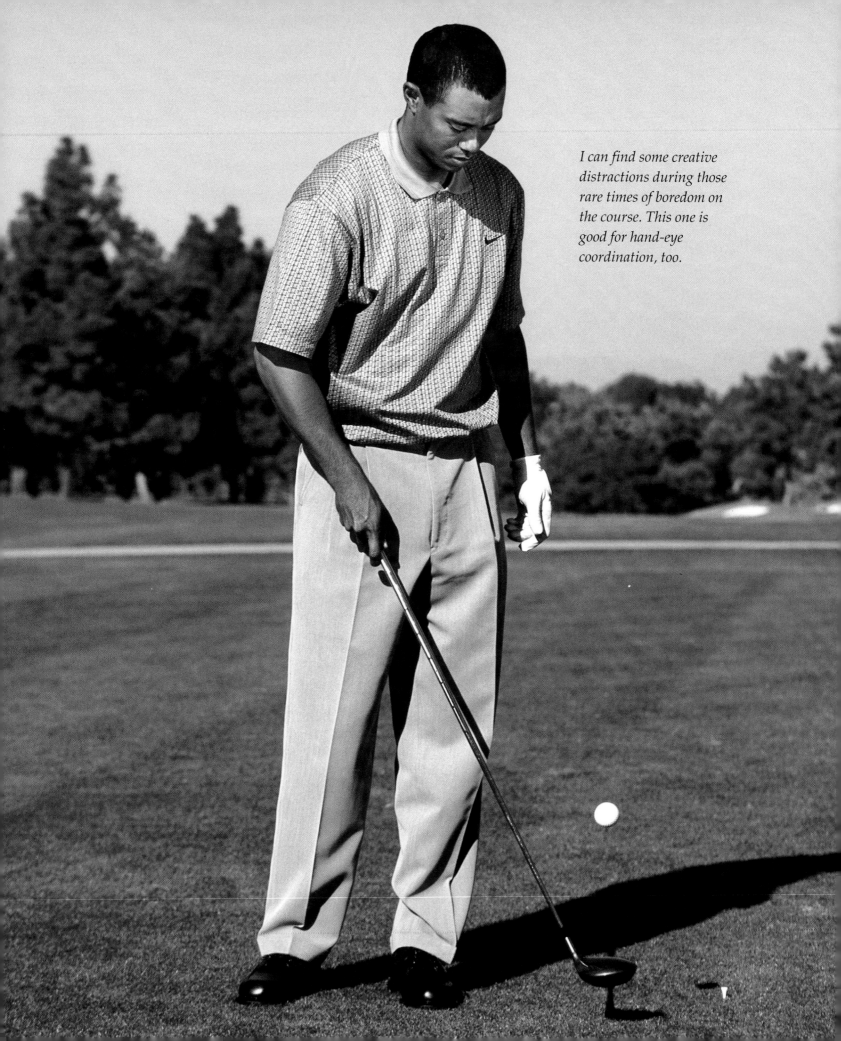

I can find some creative distractions during those rare times of boredom on the course. This one is good for hand-eye coordination, too.

While I was a student at Stanford University, my putter often gave me sweet success.

wonder whether the effort is worth it. It took me a while to understand why some days you have it and others you don't. Fact is, every day your body feels a little different and golf is such a finite game that a little off can translate into a lot. One or two degrees here and there can mean from four to seven yards. That's not a whole lot but it's magnified due to the precision the game demands. We've all had one of those frustrating days. The final round of the 1996 NCAAs at The Honors

Course in Ooltewah, Tenn., was one I'll never forget. I struggled all week, even though I shot some great numbers. I just didn't feel comfortable with my swing. I didn't have the club in the right position, but I was getting away with it because my chipping was great and I made every putt I looked at. I was somehow able to keep the ball in play for most of the holes and let my putter do the rest. In the final round I lost it altogether. I went to the range that morning and never hit a shot. It just

I am never afraid to celebrate my successes and good times with a display of emotion.

Disappointment is part of the game, and how I handle it defines me as a competitor.

wasn't there. Sometimes when that happens you can actually lower your expectations, go out and shoot a great round. Not this time. I played the first three rounds with smoke and mirrors and it finally caught up with me. Fortunately, I had a nine-shot lead and the 80 didn't cost me an individual championship. I felt extremely fortunate, more like a survivor than a champion.

Success in golf is finding equilibrium, accepting the fact that it is a game of ups and downs and learning something every time you tee it up. Finding that balance is a matter of trial and error. You must discover what works best for you and work diligently to maximize your potential. The difference between golf and most other sports is that anyone of average intelligence and coordination can learn to play it well. It requires a commitment to being the best that you can be. That has always been my approach to the game, for I, too, started as a blank page. Through my first teacher, my dad, the page began to fill. I absorbed as much information about the game as I possibly could. Through experimentation I started weeding out what could and could not hurt me. More important, I began to understand what worked best for me. Pop gave me many great lessons, not only about golf but also about life. His greatest advice to me was to always be myself. I pass that along to you as the first lesson in this book, which I wrote not as a panacea but as the ultimate tribute to Mom and Pop's ideal of caring and sharing. In essence, if you care for someone you'll share with them your most treasured possessions.

In this book I will share with you a lifetime, albeit a relatively short one, of knowledge about the greatest game in the world. I believe this book will assist you in attaining the deep joy and satisfaction that comes from playing the game well. I am convinced there is no game like it. In many ways it is a microcosm of life, teaching us both the

depths and heights of character. It demands integrity, promotes camaraderie, encourages good health and builds appreciation for the aesthetics. It is more than a well-struck iron or a holed putt. No, golf is not a game of perfection; it is one of reality. And keeping it real is more than a worthy goal in any endeavor.

Golf requires patience and perseverance. There are no shortcuts. Pop used to say you get out of it what you put into it. When my teacher, Butch Harmon, and I overhauled my swing during the 1998 season, Butch would sometimes have me repeat one movement for 30 minutes. I would get so tired it felt like my arms were going to fall off. But I kept at it until the move became ingrained in my muscle memory. Patience and practice

I ENJOY GIVING BACK

My mom and dad have always been my greatest teachers and biggest supporters. They have always been there for me with sound advice that has guided me through a lot of growing pains. I learned to trust and believe in them. To me, golf instruction is similar to a parent nurturing a child. I try to get a student to emulate everything I believe is fundamentally sound. It is my obligation to share my knowledge with others because that's what I was taught.

A teacher's advice is not to be taken lightly, especially when it is proven through experience.

If my giving back to a game that has given me so much helps one person, it will be a fitting legacy to those who helped me.

pay off. So will careful attention to the techniques explained within the pages of this book—techniques I believe will work for everyone seeking to get the best out of their games. *It is structured differently from other books, beginning with the green and progressing to the tee. That's how my dad taught me, from the smallest swing to the biggest.* The instruction combines visual, kinesthetic, cognitive and performance ideals for practical application by players of all ages and abilities. Interspersed throughout the text are seven secrets I have used to elevate my game, from becoming physically stronger to mentally tougher. I believe they will work for you, too.

Ultimately, golf is a journey full of learning and discovering. I hope, through this book, you'll discover your game—one that is powerful yet precise, consistent yet exciting, impervious to pressure yet yielding large doses of fun. After all, that's the real reason we play the game. Sometimes we forget that. I did once. I was a junior golfer playing in the Orange Bowl junior tournament in Miami. I had the lead going into the final round and made a double on the front nine. I still had the lead, but for some reason I lost all joy and flat-out quit. I took my second-place trophy and pouted. Pop sternly reprimanded me. That's the only time I ever quit on golf in my life. From that time on I realized what a privilege it is to play. And I never again lost sight of why I fell for the game in the first place.

We still try because we must.

Finding a great instructor and working my butt off to improve took my game to another level.

THE
SHORT
GAME

❖ ❖ ❖

*It wasn't by accident that
I learned to play golf from the
green back to the tee.*

At my first Masters in 1995, while still a student at Stanford, I was in for a surprise on the first green.

❖1❖
HOW TO PUTT

ROLLING THE ROCK

I came to my first Masters Tournament in 1995 thinking I could putt. Proud of my hat representing Stanford, where I was completing my freshman year, I was full of confidence. Like a lot of 20-year-olds, I had never seen a putt I didn't like. As a junior and college player, I could go deep when my putter got hot. I'd had 21 putts for 18 holes several times, and under pressure it seemed like I never missed. The length of the putt was irrelevant; I would just get up there and bang the ball hard into the hole. I was aggressive, confident and had the touch to back it up.

But I was in for a pretty rude awakening that Thursday at Augusta National. On the first hole on the first day, I stood over a 20-footer for birdie that I just knew I was going to make. It was raining and misty, the kind of conditions that tend to slow the greens down. A little voice told me to give the putt a little extra nudge; the practice green had been a touch slow by Masters standards, and I was determined to play aggressively. So I put a nice smooth stroke on the ball, accelerating the putter a bit faster through impact.

The ball rolled nicely and slowed as it neared the hole. But it didn't stop. It trickled three feet past the hole, paused for a moment, then kept going, gathering speed as it went along. Next thing I knew, the ball had rolled completely off the green. Even then, it didn't stop. Suddenly the gallery was parting to give the ball room to roam. By the time the ball stopped, I was farther from the hole than when I started and facing a very difficult recovery shot. It was a pretty startling moment. Even my playing partner, defending champion Jose Maria Olazabal, looked surprised. Though I was a bit shaken, I was determined to recover. I chipped the ball to 15 feet, and made that putt for a bogey. But right then I knew I had a lot to learn.

The more I examine putting, the more fascinating it becomes. I'm at least as captivated by putting as I am by the full swing. That's why I practice putting so much. I enjoy the process of altering my stroke a little when it gets out of kilter. I like the challenge of improving my touch, and the feeling I sometimes get when I know I can lag a fast, double-breaking 40-footer to within a foot of the hole—or else hole it. There is, and always will be, room for improvement. I guess that deep inside, I'm still 20 years old and feel I can make every putt I look at. The goal, even if it isn't a realistic one, is to putt my very best every day.

A great way to improve your feel is to putt with your eyes closed. After each putt, try to guess how far the ball rolled. This is the best drill for distance control I know of.

THE ALL-AMERICAN GRIP

I see so many types of putting grips on the pro tours these days, it gives the impression there is no "right" way to hold the putter. Maybe there isn't. The main thing in putting, whether it's with your grip, posture, stance or ball position, is to be comfortable. The putting stroke is not a very complicated action. My hands move only a foot at most in either direction during the stroke. My arms move less than that, my body less still and my head not at all. So the biggest priority in gripping the club is to establish a feeling of sensitivity, comfort and relaxation.

My putting grip is conventional in almost every way. If you look at the long history of the game and its greatest players, most of them have held the club very similarly to the way I do. I'm glad I had them as models when I was young.

IF UNIQUE IS WHAT YOU SEEK

The handle of the putter runs under the butt of my left hand. Most players like the handle running straight up the palm so the club-shaft is parallel to the left forearm. My grip is unique this way, but I believe it gives me a little extra feel and gives me freedom in my wrists when I need it.

STRAIGHT BY THE BOOK

■ A bracelet I used to wear, given to me by a Buddhist monk.

■ The back of my left hand faces the target. This "weak" position discourages the hand from rotating excessively during the stroke.

■ The back of my right hand is parallel to my left hand. I don't want my hands fighting each other during the stroke. By placing both hands square to the target, it's much easier to keep the face of the putter square during the stroke, at impact especially.

■ The reverse-overlap grip, with the left forefinger laid across the fingers of the right hand, provides a sense of unity. It doesn't lock the hands together in any way, but it does prevent either hand from becoming too dominant during the stroke.

■ My right thumb extends down the shaft to a point just below my right forefinger. Any farther and my right hand and wrist tighten a bit and don't hinge freely. Any shorter and I sacrifice control.

■ I position both thumbs directly down the top of the handle. The thumbs are as sensitive as the fingers and provide the greatest amount of feedback as I swing the putter back and through the ball.

GRIP PRESSURE: EASY DOES IT

. . . .

I was on the practice green with Butch Harmon one day in 1998 when Butch noticed something. "If you hold that putter any tighter, you're going to twist the grip right off it," he said with a laugh. I always listen to Butch and sure enough, I was holding the putter so firmly that I was squeezing the blood out of the tips of my fingers at address. I tried to hold the putter more lightly, but I didn't seem to have the same amount of control. And even then Butch said

my grip pressure was much too intense.

A few days later, Butch showed up with a device he attached to the grip of the putter. He fooled with the setting for a minute, then challenged me to hit some putts without making the device emit a loud "beep." It went off the minute I addressed the ball. I lightened my grip pressure to quiet the thing, but when I actually went to hit a putt it went off again. Man, that thing drove me crazy. But eventually, I was able to hit putts without activating the beeper. Surprisingly, I putted pretty well with that new, light grip pressure.

Still, I wanted some reassurance that holding the club lightly was the way to go. Early in 1999, at the Byron Nelson Classic, I ran into Ben Crenshaw, who may be the greatest putter of all time. I asked him how tightly he held the putter. Ben said he gripped his putter so lightly it almost fell from his hands. "The lighter you hold it, the better you'll be able to feel the weight of the putterhead at the other end of the shaft," he said.

Hearing that from Ben did it for me. I committed myself to easing my grip pressure, and it really paid off. I shot 63-64 over the weekend and won the tournament.

HOW LIGHT IS LIGHT?

I'd say that on a scale of 1 to 10, my grip pressure is about a 5. That may be tighter than Ben holds his putter, but it's pretty light for me and I do have an increased sense of feel.

If you're having trouble on lag putts, or if your speed isn't right on shorter, breaking putts, or if you feel you're manipulating the putter, check your grip pressure. No doubt about it, light is right.

PERFECT YOUR POSTURE

. . . .

With putting, little things can make a big difference. One of the fundamentals sacred to me is posture. That applies not only to how I position my body mechanically, but also in the degree of relaxation I feel before I take the putter back.

I believe in standing fairly tall at address. That enables me to see the overall line to the hole better than when I'm stooped over close to the ground. What's more, it allows my arms to hang from my shoulder sockets in a loose, comfortable manner. That reduces tension right away. My arms also have more room to swing back and through during the stroke.

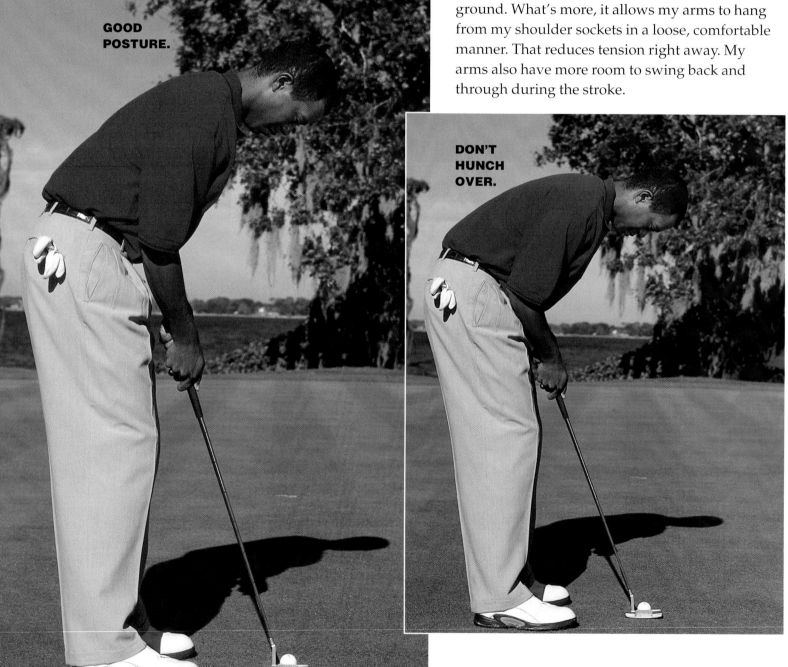

GOOD POSTURE.

DON'T HUNCH OVER.

STANCE: IT'S UP TO YOU

· ·

Because there's so little movement in your legs and torso during the stroke, the width of your stance is more a matter of comfort than anything else. Some players feel a wider stance gives them a feeling of stability and stops them from swaying. Others feel a narrow stance helps them stand more erect and gives them a better view of the line. I've varied my stance width over the years and have putted well with both a narrow stance and a wider one.

A lot of players accept the idea that they will have good days and bad days on the greens and therefore don't work at it. In fact, study and practice produce results.

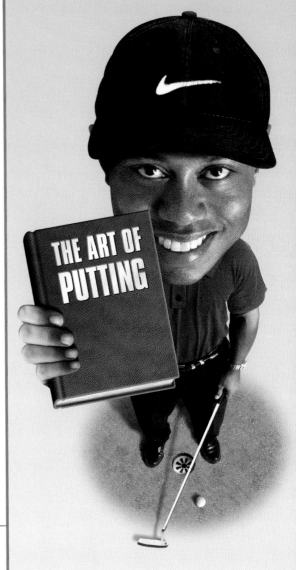

POSITION YOUR EYES DIRECTLY OVER BALL.

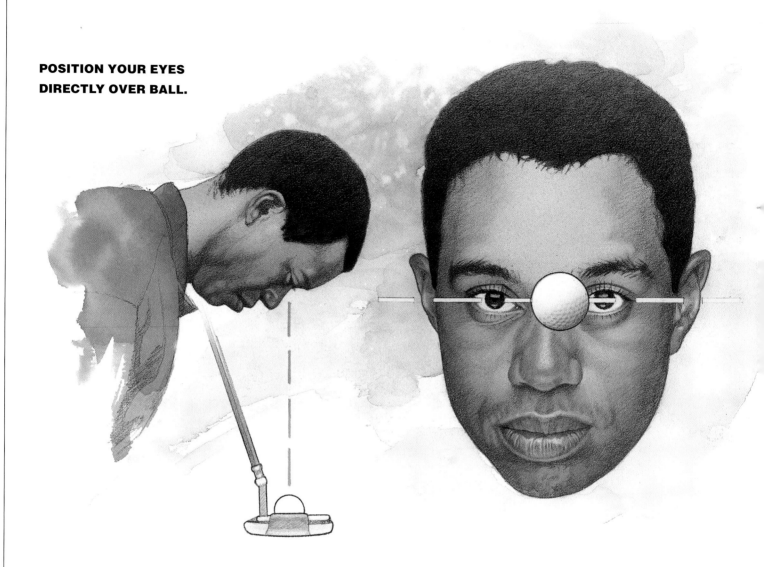

FOCUS ON YOUR EYES

· ·

The position of your eyes relative to the ball and the putting line is crucial. When I'm having trouble starting the ball on the correct line, I examine several factors.

■ Ideally, I want my eyes directly over the ball at address. It indicates I am standing the proper distance from the ball, my posture is good and I

have a dependable view of the line I want the ball to roll on. If I err, it's better to position my eyes slightly inside the line. If my head is perched out beyond the ball, I'll pull a lot of putts to the left or else have to manipulate the putterhead during the stroke to make it track on line.

■ It's acceptable to set the head and eyes a little to the right of the ball (for a right-hander like me)

YOUR EYES SHOULD BE PARALLEL TO LINE OF PUTT.

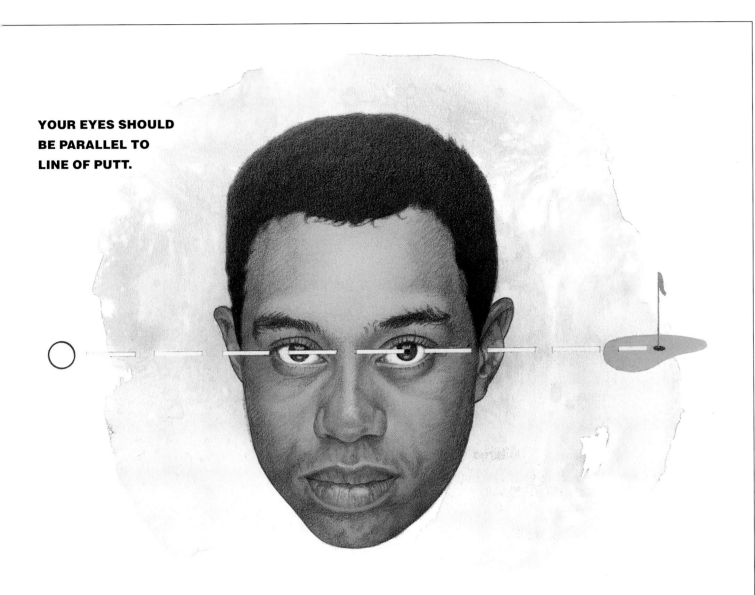

at address. In fact, it's hard not to do that if the ball is positioned ahead of center a little, which is where most players like it. My eyes are a couple of inches to the right of the ball when I look down; it gives me a view of the hole that is similar to sighting a rifle. What I don't want to do is position my head and eyes farther up the target line than the ball itself.

■ I always make sure my eyeline is parallel to the target line. If I cock my head to the left or right at address even slightly, I'll subconsciously steer the putterhead in the direction my eyes are aligned. I like to use the bill of my cap as a reference point. If the bill of my cap is parallel to the target line, I know my eyes are parallel also—provided I put my cap on straight!

SAME ROUTINE, WITHOUT FAIL

. . . .

A good putting stroke requires smooth rhythm and a steady, repeating pace. One of the secrets to accomplishing that is to do everything else smoothly and repetitively, too. I'm talking about my preputt routine, or the series of things I do before I actually pull the trigger with the putter. Regardless of your routine—and there are a lot of variations—the key is to perform it exactly the same way on every single putt.

The thing about my routine is, I never change it. I do it at the same speed and go through the same thought process every single time. Not

*Here's my routine: (**A**) I take a general view of the putt while standing behind the ball; (**B**) walk to the hole, taking a side view of the line to help determine slope; (**C**) examine the area around the hole; (**D**) walk back to my ball and crouch behind it, getting the most telling view of speed and break; (**E**) stand alongside my ball and make two practice strokes; (**F**) move the putter behind the ball and then shift my feet forward; (**G**) take two more looks at the line and hole; and (**H**) stroke the putt.*

only do I gather all the information I need about the putt itself, I also get myself in the best frame of mind to stroke the putt. By the time I take the putter back, I'm in a great flow, physically and mentally. That's what a good routine does for me and can do for you.

My preputt routine gets under way with a careful examination of topographical features on and around the green.

■ If there's a pond nearby, I know the ball will tend to break toward it.

■ If I'm playing a mountain course, I know the ball will tend to break away from the tallest peak in the vicinity.

Only after taking those general factors into account do I begin studying the line of the putt. To save time, I do much of my preputt routine unobtrusively while others are putting.

SAME PACE, BACK
AND THROUGH

· ·

From the time I was a little kid—and I mean about 4 years old—my dad hammered home the idea of swinging the putter back and through at the same speed. When you see a putting stroke that looks smooth, it's because the putter is taken back at a slow, even pace and then swung forward at the same speed. If I can stroke the ball from start to finish deliberately and with a sense of rhythm, it is much easier to keep the clubhead moving along the proper path and maintain a clubface that is square to that path from start to finish. I want to avoid any sudden change in clubhead speed, especially on the forward stroke.

LET YOUR
DOMINANT HAND
RUN THE SHOW

· ·

Although both hands are charged with swinging the putter back and through at an even pace, my dominant hand has a special responsibility. If you're right-handed, you obviously have better feel in that hand than you do in your left. Therefore, you want to instill a sense of pace with that hand especially, so it won't play too big a role in your putting stroke.

I like to hit putts with my right hand only, making sure I incorporate the same amount of pace as when I'm putting with both hands. I allow my right wrist to hinge just a bit on the backstroke and then release a little through impact. But I never allow my right wrist to "unhinge" any farther than where I had it at address. Remember, your hand leads, the clubhead trails behind.

The putter feels heavier when you hold it with one hand rather than two. Still, by holding the putter very lightly, you'll get the sense that the putter is swinging back and through almost by itself, with very little effort from your right hand.

The style of putter you use is irrelevant. The important thing is to choose a putter that hefts well in your hands and gives you a feeling of confidence just looking at it.

ALL IS WELL
AT ADDRESS.

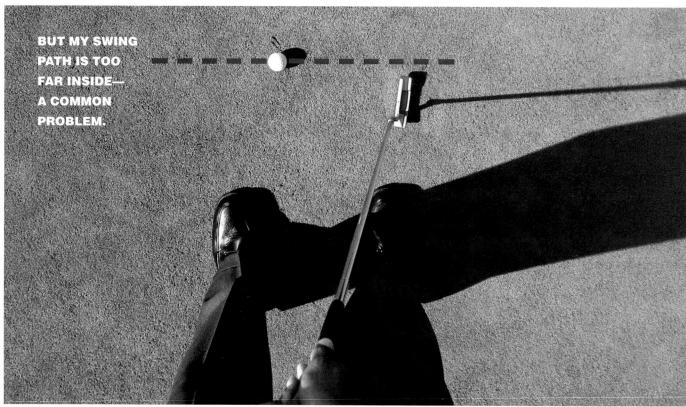

BUT MY SWING
PATH IS TOO
FAR INSIDE—
A COMMON
PROBLEM.

THE IMPORTANCE OF SWING PATH

Once I align the face of the putter square to the target line, the most important thing is to return the clubface to that position at impact. The best way to do that is to swing the putter straight back and straight through along the same path. Speaking from personal experience, that's easier said than done. On the practice green one day, Butch told me I was swinging the putter back on an inside path. I had been putting poorly and this was the reason. Butch explained that when the putter goes back on the inside, you are forced to "release" the putterhead aggressively through impact in order to get it back to square. That causes a lot of pulls to the left and pushes to the right, not to mention inconsistent speed control.

Butch cured me fast with a little drill.

Standing to my right, down the target line, he reached forward with his own putter and placed the clubhead to the inside of the line. "Now hit the putt," he said. I did, and my putterhead collided with his on the backswing. I tried it again—same thing. It took some effort, but I finally got the putter moving straight away from the ball. I started putting better almost instantly.

The straight-back-and-through path is especially important on putts of five feet or less, where I'm not hitting the ball very hard. On longer putts, where I'm forced to turn my shoulders more in order to take the putter back farther, the putterhead tends to move to the inside a little. That's fine; I'd have to separate my arms from my body too much to keep the putter moving along the straight-back path.

FOR A LONGER PUTT, THIS IS MORE LIKE IT—SLIGHTLY INSIDE, BUT NOT MUCH.

I REGULATE DISTANCE BY VARYING THE LENGTH OF MY STROKE, NOT BY APPLYING A SUDDEN BURST OF SPEED WITH MY HANDS.

SIX KEYS TO PURE PUTTING

. . . .

■ *Same Length, Back and Through*

An important key to pace and rhythm is to make my backstroke and forward stroke the same length. If I take the putter back only a few inches on a 20-footer, I'll have to accelerate suddenly to get the ball to the hole, and I'll have to lengthen my follow-through as a result.

■ *Shoulders and Arms Do Most of the Work*

The main source of movement is in the shoulders and arms. They act together; I don't want my arms running away from my shoulders at any time, in the backstroke especially. I want to keep my hands quiet during the entire stroke.

■ *Let Your Wrists Hinge—a Little*

Nothing is worse than a putting stroke that is all hands. There is too much play in the putterhead that way, and a handsy stroke doesn't hold up well under pressure. I like to keep my hands and wrists subdued during the stroke.

I don't want to freeze my hands and wrists entirely, however. If my grip pressure is light (as it should be), there is bound to be a tiny amount of hinging in my wrists. That's especially true on lag putts, where I need a longer stroke and more clubhead speed to get the ball to the hole. But keep in mind, I want to use my hands only as much as is absolutely necessary.

Arms and Putter Act as One

I want the clubshaft and my left forearm to form a straight, continuous line. To do that, I simply arch my wrists downward a little at address. By eliminating an angle between my forearms and the clubshaft, the putter will do exactly what my arms do during the stroke. The idea is to eliminate unwanted angles and levers, so the stroke is more of a one-piece action.

Keep a Steady Head

Every good putter keeps the head absolutely still from start to finish. Every bad putter I know moves the head to some degree. It's as simple as that. If I move my head even a fraction, it's almost impossible to keep my putting path stable and true. It's hard to hit the ball solidly, too. More than likely I'll open my shoulders on the forward stroke, causing me to pull the putter across the ball from out to in. I practice keeping my head dead still until well after the ball is gone.

No Peeking!

If you're like me, you can't wait to see if the ball is tracking toward the hole right after the ball leaves the putterface. But the urge to glance up too soon has some nasty consequences. The tendency to peek too soon causes my head to move and leads to sloppy contact. Not only that, if I'm distracted by thoughts of where the ball is going, I won't focus on my main job, which is to keep the putter moving directly down the target line.

I found an effective way to fight the problem: I practice putting with my left eye closed, so I can't see the target line at all with my peripheral vision. That makes it easier to keep my eyes looking straight down.

NEVER FORCE THE ISSUE

. . . .

Putting is largely about touch. To really get a feel for speed, the stroke should be as easy, smooth and natural as I can make it. If I putt like a robot, stiff, locked up and too mechanical, I won't judge distance very well, especially on longer putts.

YES

NO

Let the Toe Pass the Heel

If I keep my left arm fairly close to my side on the forward stroke, the putterhead will tend to rotate to the left after impact, the toe of the club passing the heel. I don't fight that natural tendency. The important thing is for the putterface to be square to the target line at impact, and that will happen as long as my release is smooth and unhurried.

Don't "Block It" Down the Line

Some players are so desperate to avoid pushes and pulls that they shove the putterhead down the target line, keeping the clubface dead square from start to finish. It's a very unnatural action. It doesn't do much to provide square contact, and it's almost impossible to impart the right speed consistently.

than drawing your hands and arms inward toward your body through impact.

The Left-to-Right Putt: The key to this putt is to allow the putter to "release," or rotate freely, through impact. That's harder than it sounds. The tendency is to let the putterhead drift to the right (toward the hole) through impact. The result: A miss on the low side. Keep your head down, trust your line, and let the putter release naturally.

HANDLING BREAKING PUTTS

The Right-to-Left Putt: Most right-handed players prefer a putt that breaks from right to left. That's because the arms and hands are moving outward, away from the body, through impact. It's a bit more natural to stroke the ball this way, rather

LAGGING THE LONG ONES CLOSE

• • • • • • • • • • • • • • • • • • • •

The only time I welcome a long putt is when I've reached a long par 5 in two. Nevertheless, I face putts of 40 feet or longer a lot more often than that, once per round on average at least. The goal, of course, is to avoid three-putting. Three-putts are killers, and that doesn't say anything about four-putting, which I've done a few times since I was a kid. (But I'm glad to say I've never five-putted!)

My goal is to lag my first putt dead to the hole, so I have nothing more than a tap-in left. That's setting the bar pretty high, but it's rare that I face a long putt so difficult that I can't lag it up there close. There are exceptions, of course. On the 17th hole at Augusta National during the Masters, they often cut the hole on the left side of the green on Sunday. That part of the green slopes severely from left to right. If I stop my approach shot on the left side of the green, forget it. I can't hit my first putt within eight feet—unless I hole it.

◄ *I make my backswing and forward stroke the same distance.* That's the best way to assure a smooth, rhythmic stroke with plenty of feel. If my follow-through is a bit longer than my backswing, fine. But if it's shorter, I've more than likely decelerated the putter through impact, a sure killer.

◄ *I swing the putter at the same pace, back and through.* It's important that the putter be gaining speed as it strikes the ball. But if I can feel that my putterhead is traveling at the same speed from start to finish, I'll accelerate through impact without thinking about it.

▲ *I make practice strokes while looking at the hole.* Concentration. I see in my mind's eye the length of stroke necessary to impart the right amount of speed.

▼ *A long putt is rarely perfectly flat.*
Am I putting uphill or downhill?
As I approach the green, I look
closely to determine which
side is higher.

◀ *I hit the putt solidly at all costs.*
If I miss the sweet spot of the putterface by half an
inch—which is easy to do when I'm making an extra-
long stroke—I can lose 10 feet of roll or more.

▲ *Am I putting into the grain
or downgrain?*
If I'm putting down the grain,
I can often factor in a few
extra feet of roll.

▲ *I study the last six feet of the putt closely.*
Knowing the way the ball behaves when
it's dying at the hole is crucial.

◀ *I don't forget the break!*
I can judge the speed perfectly,
but if I push or pull the putt five
feet, I haven't done myself
any favors.

▲ *When putting up or down a tier,
I divide the putt into two sections.*
It's important that the ball arrive at the
beginning of a downhill tier with just the
right speed, and conversely, that it arrive
at the top of an uphill tier with enough
speed to get the ball to the hole.

TIGER TALE:
WHAT YOU SEE IS WHAT YOU GET

The most memorable putt of my career remains the 30-footer I buried at Pumpkin Ridge on my way to winning my third straight U.S. Amateur Championship in 1995. In the 36-hole final against Steve Scott, I stood 1 down with two holes to play. My approach shot to the 17th hole was just so-so and left me a birdie putt of about 30 feet. I read the putt carefully and was certain it would break five inches to the right. Rarely have I felt so self-assured that a putt would behave exactly as I saw it. The moment I struck the putt, I knew I had started it on line. And when it dove into the hole, I was excited but not really surprised. I'm not sure there's a strong moral to that story, except that it pays to learn how to read greens.

Reading greens is a science in that you must take into account physical factors such as the slope of the green and the type of grass you're putting on. But it's an art, too. Having competed on courses all over the world, I've experienced tremendous variations in terrain, weather, agronomy and course conditioning. They all influence how the ball rolls. Here are some rules of thumb:

■ *Fast Early, Slow Late.* Grass grows quickly—enough that the same putt you hit at 8 A.M. can be considerably slower at 5 P.M. As with all rules, however, there are exceptions. When I won the 2000 U.S. Open at Pebble Beach, the greens got quicker as the day wore on. In the morning the greens were damp and therefore slow, but when the wind came up (as it usually does), the greens dried out and got a lot faster.

■ *Learn to Read Grain.* Grass doesn't grow straight up, it tends to grow toward one side or the other. Grain isn't as big a factor as it used to be because greens are cut so short nowadays. Still, it's a factor, especially on Bermuda grass. Study the hole. One side will be shaggier than the other; a ball moving in the direction of the shaggy side will travel faster than one rolling against it. Another general rule: Grass grows toward the setting sun.

■ *Wind Can Matter.* When it's blowing more than 15 m.p.h., pay attention. A golf ball weighs only a little more than an ounce and a half, so you can bet it can be influenced by the wind.

■ *Balls Roll Where Water Drains.* If there's a pond near the green, I can be sure the ball will favor moving in that direction.

■ *Mountains Are Mystifying.* If I'm playing a mountain course, strange things can happen. Putts that appear straight will break for no apparent reason. The rule: Find the highest mountain peak in the vicinity; the green will tend to slope away from it.

NARROW YOUR WORLD

• •

A few years ago, I started cupping my hands around my eyes while I read putts. The reason I do it is not because I see more, it's because I see less. The PGA Tour can get some pretty big galleries, and there's always a lot of movement I sometimes find distracting. By forming a little tunnel with my hands, I can focus totally on reading my line.

You probably don't have too big a crowd watching you play, but still there are distractions—carts zooming around, fellows walking around the greens and so forth. If you have trouble concentrating, try my "tunnel vision" technique. It will sharpen your focus and help you hole more putts.

·2·
HOW TO
GET IT DOWN

TURNING THREE INTO TWO

I don't think I've ever felt more pressure than the day our Western High School golf team was going up against our big crosstown rival to decide our district championship. We were playing at Los Coyotes Country Club in Buena Park, Calif., a nice course that has played host to the LPGA Tour. Our matches were only nine holes and were played at stroke play, with everybody's score counting. I was playing well and came to the last hole four under par. But the match was very close. When I saw my coach and teammates gathered around the par-3 ninth green, I knew what I did on that hole could very possibly spell the difference between our team winning or losing.

My tee shot sailed over the green, leaving me a tricky little downhill pitch from light rough. My ball was sitting up nicely. I figured I would have no trouble hitting a little flop shot up close to the hole, from where I would make the putt for par and lead my team to glory.

I addressed the ball with my sand wedge, opening my stance and the clubface. Taking a deep breath, I made a healthy-sized backswing, cut across the ball firmly—and whiffed the shot. My lie, as it turned out, had been too good. The clubhead had slid right under the ball.

Now I faced an even more difficult shot, because the ball had settled lower into the rough. Feeling more angry than scared, I settled over the ball again and played the same type of shot, a high-risk flop. This time I holed it out! I saved a par and our team pulled out the title.

Two lessons were driven home to me that afternoon, lessons my dad had pounded into my head for years. The first is, a good short game can save a round regardless of how poorly you're hitting the ball from tee to green. The second lesson had to do with that whiff. That terrible shot, where I failed to judge the quality of the lie correctly, made it clear that I could never reach my full potential unless I built a reliable short game.

As you'll see, there's more to getting up and down than you may think.

THE STATS TELL THE STORY

The thing I'll remember about my 2000 season was that I performed well in all facets of my game. Not having any really weak areas was the reason I won eight tournaments, was the leading

I missed hitting in regulation, I made par or better on two of them from all kinds of tough situations around the greens. If I had stumbled in that category, it would have cost me a few tournaments, the Vardon Trophy and a whole bunch of money.

money-winner, took home three major championships, won the Vardon Trophy for low stroke average, and was named Player of the Year. But it was my short game that made the biggest contribution.

I ranked first in the Greens In Regulation category, hitting better than three greens out of every four with my approaches. That adds up to just under 14 greens per round, my best percentage ever.

I also ranked first in putting. That's a telling stat, because if you're hitting lots of greens and making lots of putts, you're making lots of birdies.

The Scrambling category, where I ranked third over all, was the real key and proves how important the short game is to scoring. When I missed the green, I got up and down for par or better 67.1 percent of the time. So, of the four greens per round

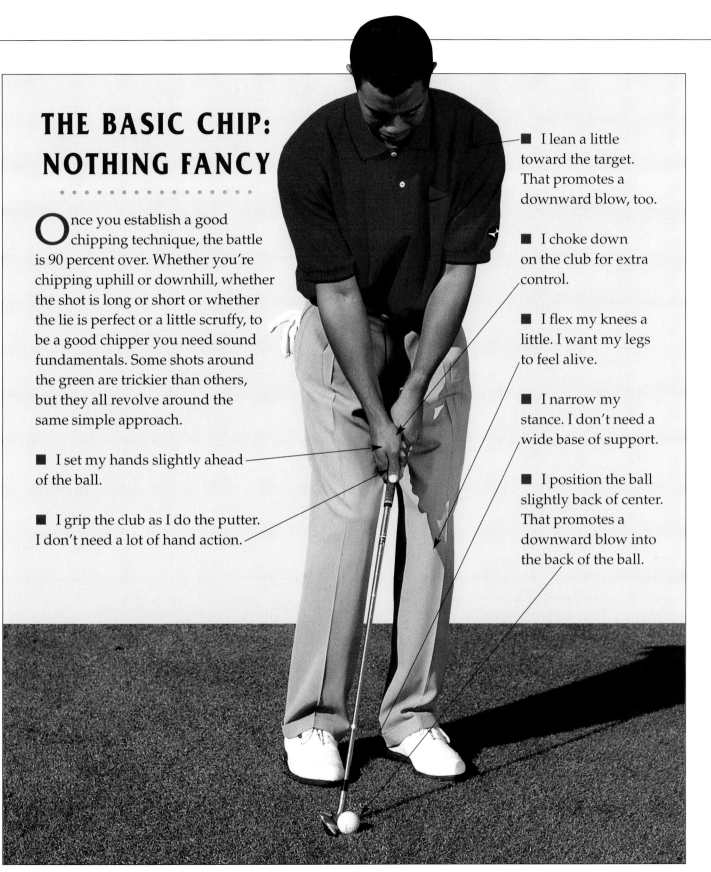

THE BASIC CHIP: NOTHING FANCY

. . . .

Once you establish a good chipping technique, the battle is 90 percent over. Whether you're chipping uphill or downhill, whether the shot is long or short or whether the lie is perfect or a little scruffy, to be a good chipper you need sound fundamentals. Some shots around the green are trickier than others, but they all revolve around the same simple approach.

■ I set my hands slightly ahead of the ball.

■ I grip the club as I do the putter. I don't need a lot of hand action.

■ I lean a little toward the target. That promotes a downward blow, too.

■ I choke down on the club for extra control.

■ I flex my knees a little. I want my legs to feel alive.

■ I narrow my stance. I don't need a wide base of support.

■ I position the ball slightly back of center. That promotes a downward blow into the back of the ball.

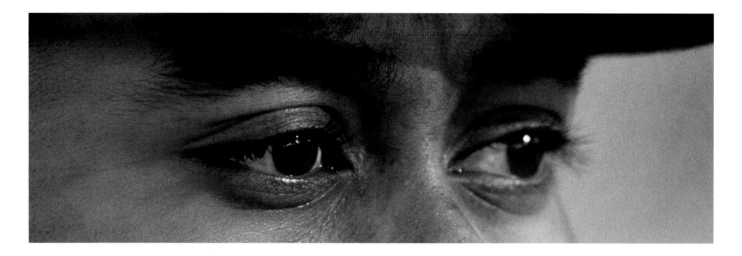

SEE THE SHOT
HAPPEN BEFORE
YOU HIT IT

· · · · · · · · · · · · · · · · · · · ·

The chip, like a putt, requires an advance "read." But I'm looking for more than how the ball will behave after it lands on the green. To control distance accurately (that's much harder to do than start the ball on line), I choose a spot where I want the ball to land, and then form a mental picture of the ball actually traveling there.

Ready to Go
■ I hold the club softly and make sure there's no tension in my arms.

■ I open my stance to the target line. I see the line better, and it helps limit action to my arms and shoulders.

■ I keep my chin held high, my back straight. A lot of bad chippers hunch down over the ball.

■ I hold the club very lightly at address.

GIVE IT THE OLD 1-2

· ·

The chipping stroke is simple. It's an easy one-two action controlled by the shoulders more than the arms and hands. You don't need much force. My goal is to hit the ball solidly, making sure the clubhead is traveling downward at the moment it strikes the ball.

■ I start the backswing with my shoulders, allowing my arms and hands to follow. I don't let my arms separate too far from my body. Tempo is important; there's no need to rush on either the backswing or forward swing.

■ At all costs, I hit down on the back of the ball. I don't try to help the ball into the air—the loft of the club will take care of that for me.

■ The stroke may be short, but it's not a stab. I try to accelerate smoothly.

■ A good thought is to return the arms to the position they were in at address. That means, my hands are ahead of the ball. No scooping!

■ I keep my eyes focused on the back of the ball. After impact, my eyes stay focused on that same point.

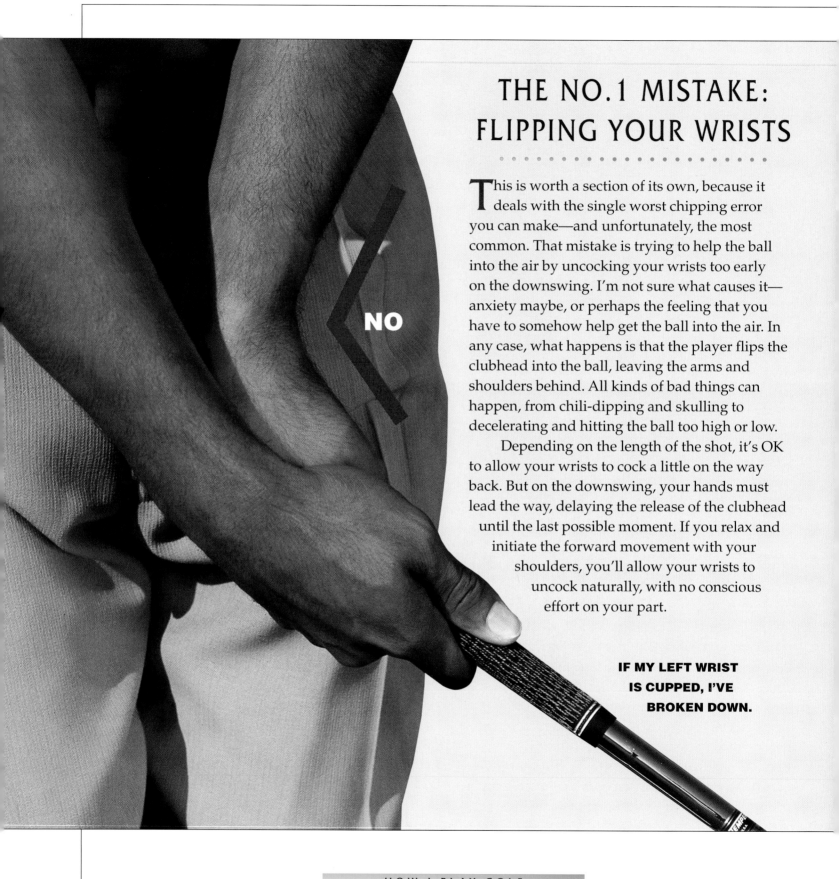

THE NO.1 MISTAKE: FLIPPING YOUR WRISTS

NO

This is worth a section of its own, because it deals with the single worst chipping error you can make—and unfortunately, the most common. That mistake is trying to help the ball into the air by uncocking your wrists too early on the downswing. I'm not sure what causes it—anxiety maybe, or perhaps the feeling that you have to somehow help get the ball into the air. In any case, what happens is that the player flips the clubhead into the ball, leaving the arms and shoulders behind. All kinds of bad things can happen, from chili-dipping and skulling to decelerating and hitting the ball too high or low.

Depending on the length of the shot, it's OK to allow your wrists to cock a little on the way back. But on the downswing, your hands must lead the way, delaying the release of the clubhead until the last possible moment. If you relax and initiate the forward movement with your shoulders, you'll allow your wrists to uncock naturally, with no conscious effort on your part.

IF MY LEFT WRIST IS CUPPED, I'VE BROKEN DOWN.

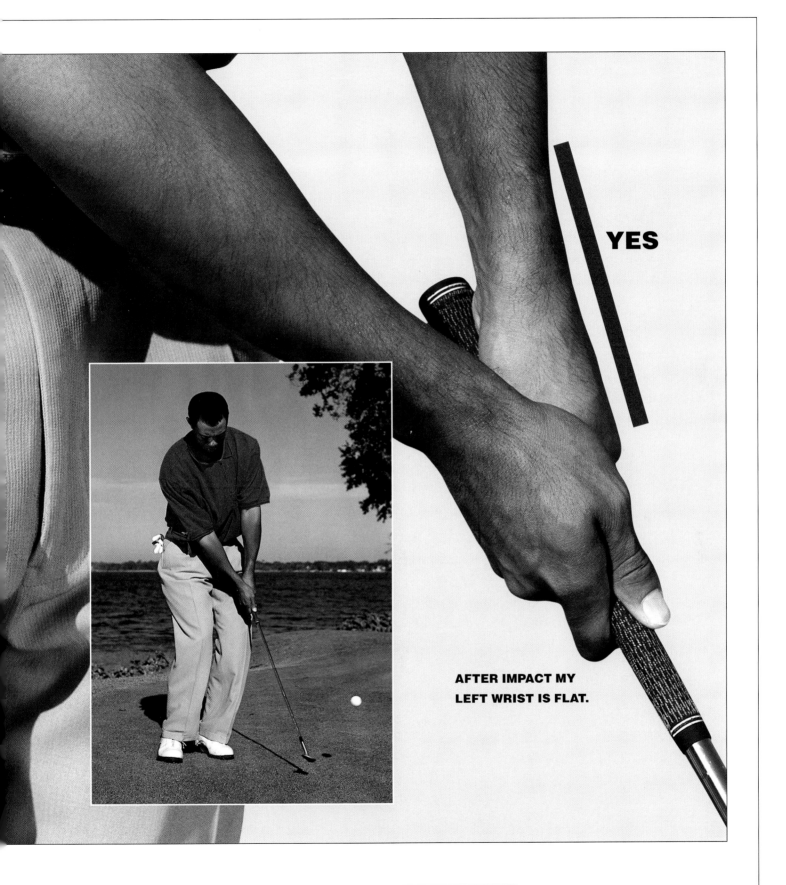

YES

AFTER IMPACT MY
LEFT WRIST IS FLAT.

TIGER TALE:
CHOOSE YOUR WEAPON WISELY

The best short-game artists vary their club selection around the greens. They vary the speed, trajectory and distance of ball flight with the club, not with the type of stroke they make. If it's a long chip that requires more roll than flight, I will choose a less-lofted club, such as a 7-iron. Shorter chips can require anything up to a 60-degree sand wedge.

Still, you probably are going to lean toward your favorite chipping club. My personal choice is my 56-degree sand wedge. At the 1998 Million Dollar Challenge in South Africa, I found myself locked in an intense duel against Nick Price. We both had gone low that day and had separated ourselves from the field. At one point on the back nine, Nick birdied five straight holes and I birdied four of the same five and then birdied the next. We came to the last hole with me trailing by one stroke.

Nick hit the green on that last hole and I didn't, although I was closer to the hole than he was. Nick two-putted for his par and now it was my turn— hole the chip and enter a playoff, or miss and take the long plane ride home. My ball was in the fringe 30 feet from the hole, sitting perfectly with a beautiful run to the hole. I really could have used any club for that shot—an 8-iron came to mind, then a pitching wedge, then my trusty sand wedge. All things being equal, I preferred my sand wedge. I just like the look and feel of it. I chose a spot on the green to land the ball, went through my routine, got set and hit the ball perfectly. It landed on the spot I had chosen, hopped once, started rolling and took the little right-to-left break perfectly. It dove into the middle of the hole and we played off for the title—which incidentally, was worth more than a million dollars.

Nick, unfazed by my chip, won that playoff. But my point is, don't be afraid to have a small bias toward your favorite chipping club. As long as your favorite club can deliver the correct type of shot, you're allowed to deviate from the norm.

HOW TO HANDLE GREENSIDE ROUGH

. . . .

Tall grass around the greens intimidates most golfers, and understandably so. For me it's one of the hardest shots there is, though I've gotten much better at it. At the 2000 U.S. Open at Pebble Beach, I landed in the tall stuff a few times, but managed to save par almost every time.

■ I use my 60-degree wedge. The tall grass tends to close the clubface, and I need all the loft I can get.

■ I distribute 60 percent of my weight on my forward foot—the one closest to the green. That encourages a steep, knifelike angle of attack with the clubhead.

■ I hold the club more firmly than normal, especially with my left hand. Again, the rough will try to twist the clubface closed.

■ I make a very upright backswing, cocking my wrists abruptly.

■ On the downswing, the force of the clubhead should be expended *downward*, to penetrate the grass. I don't let the clubhead approach the ball on a level angle; I'd be at the mercy of the rough.

■ I restrict my follow-through. In fact, if I hit down sharply, there won't *be* any follow-through.

THE 3-WOOD CHIP: A FOOLPROOF TECHNIQUE

B utch Harmon taught me this shot early in the week of the 1996 U.S. Open at Oakland Hills, and I can't think of one that had a bigger immediate impact on my game. The first time I tried it, on the

18th hole of the third round, I actually holed the shot. At Quad Cities later that year, I holed out using the 3-wood chip three times. It's a much easier shot to play than most players would think.

When to Play the Shot

The 3-wood chip is a good choice when your ball is in the fringe or in short, light rough around the green. It's effective because the broad sole of the 3-wood will resist getting snagged by the rough near impact. What's more, the 3-wood has enough loft to carry the ball a few feet onto the green, from where it rolls like a putt the rest of the way to the hole. Don't try this shot if your ball is sitting down in deep rough. Size up the situation carefully before you grab that lofted wood from your bag.

"Pop" the Clubface Into the Ball

I keep my left hand relaxed. I take the clubhead away from the ball low, so it brushes the top of the grass. I use my wrists to pop the clubface into the back of the ball, keeping the back of my left hand moving down the target line. I don't feel like I'm jabbing at the ball with the clubhead. I just accelerate the clubhead more quickly than usual. The worst thing you can do is let the clubhead slow down just before impact.

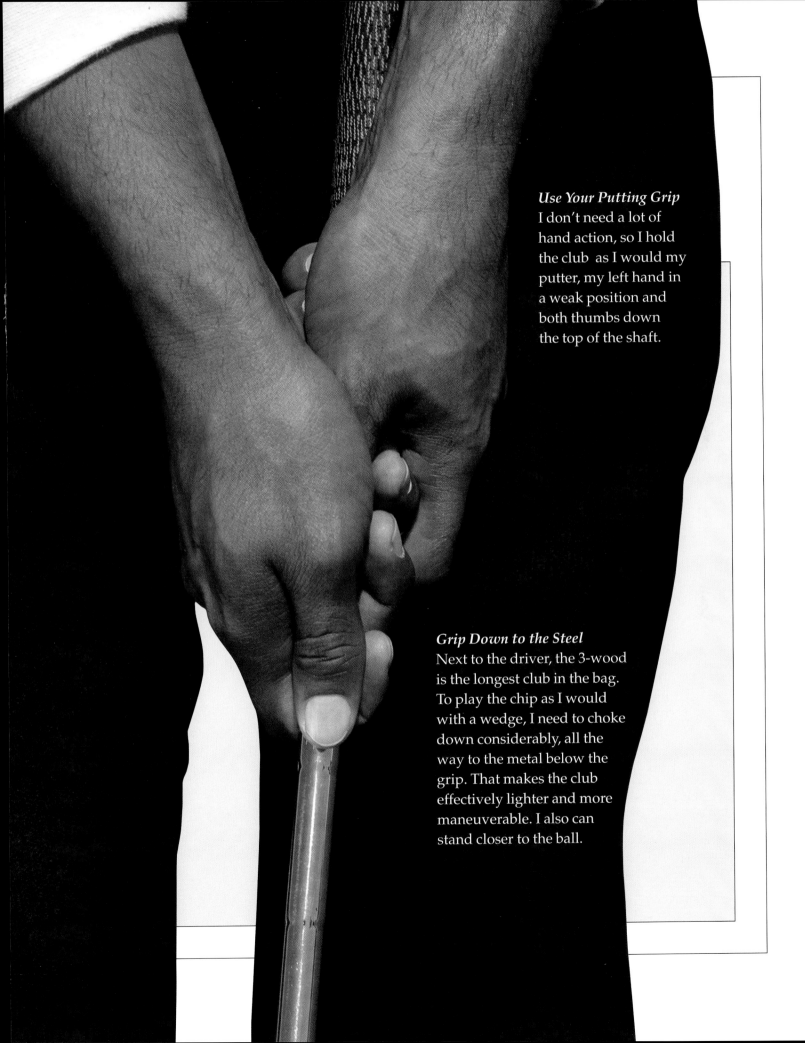

Use Your Putting Grip
I don't need a lot of hand action, so I hold the club as I would my putter, my left hand in a weak position and both thumbs down the top of the shaft.

Grip Down to the Steel
Next to the driver, the 3-wood is the longest club in the bag. To play the chip as I would with a wedge, I need to choke down considerably, all the way to the metal below the grip. That makes the club effectively lighter and more maneuverable. I also can stand closer to the ball.

THE SIMPLE PITCH

The pitch is not a long shot, but it requires a lot more hand, arm and body action than the chip shot. That's because you need more clubhead speed to get the ball in the air. It really is like a mini version of the full swing. Even your lower body plays a role, as the hips turn slightly back and through to accommodate the motion in your shoulders, arms and hands. It's a delicate balance; you need enough momentum to slide the club-head through the grass and under the ball, but not so much as to rocket the ball over the green.

Preprogram the Desired Loft
The secret to hitting the ball high and soft is not to force it. Four preswing adjustments will help you a lot:

1. Choose a lofted club, either your standard sand wedge or 60-degree wedge.

2. Open your stance by aligning your feet well left of the target line.

3. Open the clubface to increase loft.

4. Play the ball forward, off your left toe.

Focus on Your Hands

The hands are much more active on the pitch than on the chip. I strengthen my left-hand grip a bit by turning it to my left at address—that will enable my hands to cock more easily during the swing. It's crucial that I hold the club lightly, both for mobility and feel.

Let the Club Do the Work

The rest is easy. I pick the club up steeply on the backswing, allowing my wrists to cock naturally. Watch my tempo—I'm not making a long swing, but it still needs to be smooth and rhythmic.

Keep Everything Moving

My main downswing thought is to slide the clubhead under the ball. I make sure I accelerate—if I allow the clubhead to stop, I'll probably chunk the shot. I don't rotate my hands and the clubhead dramatically through impact. On the follow-through, the clubface should be aiming at the sky, proof I've maintained the loft of the clubface.

THE 30-YARD PUNCH

One of the hardest shots to master (and one every golfer faces virtually every round) is the short punch from about 30 yards from the green. Like any shot that requires something less than a full swing, you need good technique and a soft touch to pull it off.

I position my ball just back of center, which helps me hit down on the ball. I narrow my stance so my feet are between the width of my shoulders; I don't need a wide, stable base because I won't be making a very long swing.

I start the swing low and wide, making sure my left arm is fully extended. I always remember to turn my shoulders and hips a little, too.

BACKSWING IS
LOW AND WIDE.

ARMS ARE STILL IN FRONT OF MY BODY.

Big Muscles Guide a Short Swing

I never try to swing through the ball with my arms and hands alone, because it's too difficult to control the loft of the clubface and regulate clubhead speed. My thought is to simply unturn my hips and let them guide my shoulders, arms and hands through the downswing. A low, abbreviated finish is my goal—it proves the big muscles have directed the motion, not my arms and hands.

With this basic technique, I can play any variety of short shots. By moving my ball position forward a touch and choosing one of my sand wedges, I can loft the ball high. By playing the ball even farther back and choosing a less-lofted club, I can play the bump-and-run.

THE FLOP: MAKING THE HARD LOOK EASY

No doubt about it, the flop shot is a high-risk gamble. I only play it when I have very little green to work with or when it's the only way to get the ball close to the hole. Still, it's a shot every golfer needs to have. The nature of modern design features around many greens demands it.

When I'm chipping uphill, I usually prefer to take the flagstick out of the hole. Downhill, it's just the opposite—I leave it in so it can behave like a backstop if I chip a little strong.

I Open My Stance, Play the Ball Forward
My stance and clubface are both open at address, with the ball played off my left heel. I grip the club more lightly than normal, to promote lots of hand speed on the downswing. I like a wide stance because it forces me to execute the shot from the waist up. The swing is 90 percent shoulders, arms and hands.

Short Shot, Long Swing
On the backswing, I pick the club up steeply and cup my left wrist into a slightly concave "V"—that opens the clubface even farther, which guarantees maximum loft through impact. I make a long swing, again to help generate speed. I accelerate quickly through impact, trying to slide the club under the ball. I remember to follow through; I don't want to chop at the ball.

I Aim for the Toe of the Club

One of my tricks for making the ball land softly is to contact the ball on the toe of my 60-degree sand wedge. I still get the same high trajectory, but striking the ball out on the toe tends to deaden the shot. I can make a fairly aggressive swing without fear of catching a "flyer" that sails over the green. I can always count on the ball stopping very close to where it lands.

KNOW YOUR LIMITATIONS

. . . .

The key to succeeding at the flop shot is judging when you can—and when you can't—pull it off. I don't even try to hit the flop unless my lie is at least decent. I want to have a bit of cushion underneath the ball for the sand wedge or 60-degree wedge to slide cleanly.

No Go. *Never try the flop from hardpan or other tight lie. If you hit behind the ball even a fraction, the clubhead will bounce into the ball and skull it over the green.*

No Go. *Never try it when the ball is sitting down deeply in tall grass. The average player doesn't have the strength to plow through grass with sufficient force.*

Go! *Now we're talking. A clean lie or even a fluffy one is fine, because you can slide the clubhead under the ball without much interference. The shot is easier than it looks.*

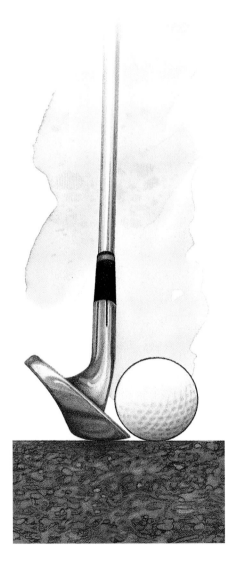
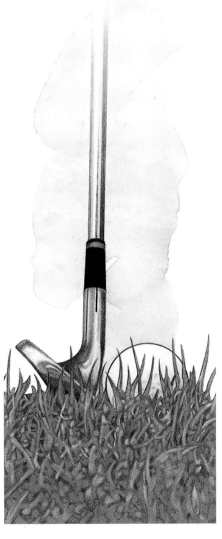

❖3❖
HOW TO ESCAPE FROM SAND

MAKING THE HARD EASY

There are tough shots, and then there was the one I had on the 16th hole at Poipu Bay Resort in Hawaii during the 1997 Grand Slam of Golf. With three holes to play, I was trailing Ernie Els by three shots and desperately needed a birdie to have even an outside chance of catching him. When I saw my approach to 16 drop into the right greenside bunker, I knew a birdie would be unlikely, but not impossible. I'd holed sand shots before.

But when I got close enough to observe my lie, I saw a shot that was close to impossible. The ball had buried into the thick, wet sand. Worse, it was on a severe downslope. To get the ball out of the bunker would be very difficult, and if I did there was no way it was going to hold the green. A thick clump of bushes beyond the green was beckoning to my ball. I was a dead man.

Or was I? A steep, grassy embankment was just beyond the bunker. If I could somehow make the ball fly directly into the embankment, the ball might release forward and get on the green. It was a 100-1 shot, but I had to try it.

I addressed the ball as though I were ready to chop wood. I didn't swing the club back so much as lift it straight in the air, then brought it down into the sand as though I were swinging an ax. I swung as hard as I could, closing my eyes tight, and hoped for the best.

When I found the courage to peek at the outcome, I saw an amazing sight. The ball had shot straight forward like a bullet and slammed into the embankment. The ball jumped into the air a good three feet and continued forward, stopping two feet from the hole. I knocked the putt in for one of the best pars of my life, and very proudly tipped my cap to the gallery. Even Ernie congratulated me. Ernie parred the hole and held on to win by three. But that sand shot, which ranks as one of the best I've ever played in my life, made my day and eased the pain of losing.

THE NO-FAIL SETUP

More than for any other shot in golf, the setup for the standard bunker shot determines the type of swing I make and the way the club behaves when it enters the sand. It's a four-part process.

I Open My Stance
I align everything—my feet, hips and shoulders—to the left of the target. That preprograms an out-to-in swing, the clubhead cutting across the sand and the ball through impact.

I Open the Clubface
I aim the clubface to the right of the target the amount you see here. That does two things: It increases the loft of the clubface so I can hit the ball high and soft, and it also increases the amount of "bounce" on the sole of the clubhead.

I Weaken My Grip
The last thing I want on a sand shot is for the clubface to rotate to a closed position through impact. To discourage that rotation, I weaken my left-hand grip at address, so the back of my left hand faces the target.

I Position the Ball Forward
I like it just opposite my left heel. Playing the ball forward promotes a higher trajectory, and also encourages me to slide the clubhead easily through the sand.

EASY DOES IT

Remember one thing: The standard bunker shot is about technique, not about strength. I don't apply any more effort than I would on a 40-yard shot from the fairway.

I Downsize My Swing

I don't need a long swing with lots of body action, as there is no need for extra distance. I keep my grip pressure light, maintain an easy rhythm and swing my hands back to about shoulder height.

I Cock My Wrists Fully

The clubhead speed I generate comes mainly from my hands and arms. I break my wrists early on the backswing and cock them all the way. This is a very "handsy" shot, with very little movement in my hips and legs.

I'm a Right-Hand Man

The swing on the greenside bunker shot is dominated by the right hand. Through impact, the action is very similar to throwing a ball.

I Go Ahead and Release

Even though I've really slung the club through the sand with my right hand, you'll notice that the toe of the clubhead hasn't turned over fully after impact. That's due to my weak left-hand grip. I know the ball will come out high and soft.

I Slide, I Don't Chop

See how the sand is being thrown forward on a fairly low angle? That's because I haven't hit down too steeply on the ball. I simply try to swing through impact into the follow-through, the ball coming out on a small cushion of sand.

HOW MUCH SAND
DO I TAKE?

The amount of sand I take depends on how much spin I want to put on the ball. I've drawn lines to indicate where the clubhead should enter the sand, which determines how much backspin I will apply. When I want the ball to run after it hits the green, I aim for a spot about three inches behind the ball. The ball then comes out on a thick cushion of sand with hardly any backspin.

When I want to hit the ball high and make it stop quickly, I'll hit maybe an inch behind the ball, sometimes less. I very rarely try to pick the ball cleanly without taking any sand at all, as the ball can very easily get away from me and fly too far.

The rules permit you to remove a man-made object (such as a cigarette butt) from the bunker, but you can't remove natural objects such as a twig or leaf.

SCRATCH
SCRATCH

WHY THE SAND WEDGE WORKS

The sand wedge has the most distinctive design of any club in the bag. It is very well-suited for sand, because the design prevents the clubhead from digging too deeply, which would cause me to flub the shot. Note the side-by-side comparison between a typical sand wedge and its closest relative, the pitching wedge.

■ The flange along the sole of the clubhead extends lower than the leading edge. That causes the club to behave like a rudder when it strikes the sand, skidding through it easily instead of penetrating too deeply.

■ The flange also is wider from back to front than the soles of the other irons. That's another reason it glides through the sand rather than digging deeply into it.

■ The sand wedge is the shortest club in the bag (except for your putter), and is also the heaviest. That extra mass helps the clubhead penetrate the sand just far enough to slide under the ball.

■ The sand wedge has more loft than any other club, anywhere from 52 degrees to more than 60. When I'm playing from a greenside bunker to a pin cut near the edge of the green, I need as much height on the shot as possible.

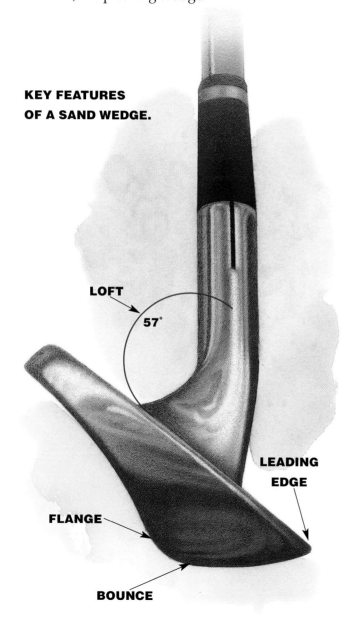

KEY FEATURES OF A SAND WEDGE.

LOFT

57°

LEADING EDGE

FLANGE

BOUNCE

I ALWAYS ACCELERATE

If there is one mistake common among poor bunker players, it's decelerating through impact. It probably stems from hitting at the ball instead of through it. To be consistent from sand, the clubhead must be gaining speed when it enters the sand instead of slowing down. This is true even on short bunker shots. I try to imagine that the club is traveling its fastest at a point six inches beyond the ball.

I GO AFTER
IT HARD WITH
MY RIGHT HAND.

A PRIMER ON THE BURIED LIE

A ball buried in sand can work on your mind. Remember that shot I pulled off from a buried lie at the Grand Slam of Golf in Hawaii? When I first saw that the ball was buried, I didn't exactly look forward to playing it. I won't lie; I was discouraged. Not only did I have an awkward stance, but the fact that the ball was buried meant I would have limited control over how the ball behaved when I hit it. I realized I would need a lot of luck just to get up and down and that a birdie was almost out of the question. It was all I could do to pull myself together and apply everything I had into playing that shot.

At first blush, buried lies bum all of us out.

Truth is, buried lies aren't all that difficult to play—if you don't count that lucky shot I pulled off in Hawaii. Sure, you won't hit the ball as close to the hole consistently as you would from a perfect lie, but you can still hit the ball close enough to have a reasonable chance at an up-and-down.

I Hit the Spot
To get the ball out of a plugged lie, I have to find a way to make the club penetrate

1.
THIS IS WHERE THE CLUB ENTERS THE SAND.

2.

**I LINE UP
TO THE
LEFT...**

3.

**AND PUNCH
DOWN
FIRMLY.**

the sand as deeply as possible. I want to take a divot that is deep enough to bury a small animal in. I like to aim for a spot about two inches behind the ball—that's where the divot starts.

I Open Up and Lean to the Left
I'm going to need a very vertical swing, the club entering the sand on as steep an angle as possible. I adjust my setup accordingly: (1) I address the ball with an open stance to encourage a steep, out-to-in swing path; (2) I lean to my left so my spine is more vertical as opposed to being slanted

to my right; (3) I open the clubface and position my hands ahead of the ball.

Forget Finesse!
This is no time to make a soft, cozy swing. I put a lot of effort into the shot, applying extra force with my right hand. Remember, I swing down as opposed to through the shot. I'll have almost no follow-through because the sand will stop the clubhead less than a foot after impact. The ball will come out with almost no spin, so I allow for extra run.

THE HARDEST SHOT IN GOLF

· · · · · · · · · · ·

No doubt about it, the toughest shot to play well consistently is the long explosion. By long, I mean a shot of about 30 yards—too long to play with your green-side bunker technique, too short to play like you would a full shot from a fairway bunker. There is an effective way to play it, but even after I show you how, you're going to need lots of practice. I experiment with different clubs, too. For a 30-yard shot I'll use anything from a sand wedge to an 8-iron depending on the lie.

I Modify My Setup
Because this shot requires as much body action as a full-swing shot from the fairway, I set up with my feet and shoulders open very slightly to the target line. I don't want to be so open that I can't turn freely, but I am open enough to make the clubhead approach the ball on a head-on path instead of from inside the target line.

Clubface Is Square, Ball Slightly Forward
Opening the clubface increases loft, and I don't want to hit the ball so high that it can't travel far enough forward to reach the green. So I set the clubface square to the target line. I also will want to take just a little sand on this shot, so I aim about an inch behind the ball (note line in sand). Precision is everything. Take more sand than that, and I'll come up short. Hit the ball thin, I'll airmail the green.

I Swing with Controlled Fury
I'll need as much clubhead speed as I can muster, so I'll want to make as big a backswing as I comfortably can. But remember what I said about precision—I make sure I keep my head still, and maintain a smooth tempo. I swing through the ball with lots of acceleration, arriving at a full, complete finish.

DIALING IN MY DISTANCE

Making the transition from a short sand shot to a longer one is pretty tricky. A lot of players regulate their distance by opening or closing the clubface, or else varying how much sand they take. I prefer to regulate how far the ball flies by adjusting the length of my follow-through. The longer the shot, the harder I try to achieve a full, complete finish. This little trick is very effective, because in order to lengthen my follow-through, I have to accelerate pretty fiercely through impact. On the other hand, a short follow-through means I haven't swung all out through impact and the ball won't travel as far.

FOR QUICK HEIGHT, MAINTAIN LOFT

One of the things I love about playing in the British Open is the unique course design features you see in Scotland and England. The most dramatic may be the steep, sod-faced bunkers that are easy to get into and brutal trying to escape from. I try to avoid these monstrosities at almost any cost, because you sometimes are forced to play sideways to get out of one, and I don't like throwing away strokes. I'm getting good at avoiding them, too—when I won the 2000 British Open at St. Andrews, I didn't land in one all week.

That wasn't the case at Carnoustie, where the British Open was played in 1999 and where the above photo was taken. The picture shows how I pulled the shot off. See how the face of my sand wedge is still facing skyward? That shows I maintained the loft of the clubface, never allowing the clubhead to turn over through impact. And look at how much sand I took. That shows the importance of penetrating the sand deeply enough for the clubhead to slide under the ball and get it up in the air.

If your lie is suspect, it's better to play the ball farther back in your stance than farther forward.

SOME EXPLOSIVE THOUGHTS

I believe the principles of good sand play are pretty much the same for everyone. If you want to hit the ball higher, there's no arguing that you must either open the clubface or position the ball farther forward in your stance to increase your launch angle. I mean, there's no other sound way to obtain more height on the shot.

There are other principles that have more to do with strategy and club selection than with physics and swing mechanics. Every amateur (high handicappers especially) should obey the following rules at all times.

■ From fairway bunkers, forget about using any club longer than a 4-iron unless the sand is moist and packed, with the ball perched in a perfect lie.

■ Another fairway bunker tip: Take at least one club more than you would from grass at the same distance.

■ The longer the shot, the lighter you should hold the club. That increases your ability to generate speed, and speed is necessary on every shot from sand.

■ If your lie is even a little dicey, position the ball at least an inch farther back in your stance than you would from a perfect lie. If the lie is bad, play it back even farther.

■ From greenside bunkers, aim for the top of the flagstick—most misses from sand come up short rather than long, so give yourself the benefit of the doubt.

TIGER TALE:
HOW TO PLAY FROM FAIRWAY BUNKERS

Some people say the best shot they've ever seen me hit was a 6-iron from a fairway bunker on the 72nd hole of the 2000 Canadian Open. I don't know about it being my best shot ever, but it definitely was one of the best I hit all year and it has to rank right up there among my most memorable sand shots. Explaining how I played it really is four lessons in one—it includes strategy, trusting your swing, proper club selection and reading the elements.

At the time I was holding on to a one-stroke lead over Grant Waite, who I just couldn't shake all day even though I was playing very well. My drive on the last hole had drifted into the fairway bunker, and I had exactly 218 yards to the pin. Grant's shot had found the fairway but he was away and would hit first. The outcome of his shot would determine whether I played safely or aggressively. When he knocked his ball on the green only 20 feet from the hole, it really forced my hand. Instead of taking a shorter club and aiming for the middle of the green, I had to take one more club and try to hit it close.

There are easier shots in golf. In addition to the distance—218 yards is a long way to hit a 6-iron even from a perfect lie in the fairway—it was raining and the wind was blowing from the left, directly toward the water that was set hard by the right side of the green. I decided on the 6-iron and aimed for the middle of the green, hoping the wind would blow the ball a little to the right.

As for how I played the shot, I had been working on a new fairway bunker technique I had discovered back home in Orlando. It consisted of my flattening my swing plane a little bit in order to shallow out my angle of approach into the ball and provide a little more margin for error. I also had weakened my left-hand grip to make sure the clubface wouldn't turn over through impact. It had worked well in practice, but practice and competition are two different things.

I decided to give that new technique a try. If not now, when? Eventually you have to put techniques to the fire to see if they hold up. And I had a lot going for me. I had a great lie, my confidence was high and I was feeling strong.

I set up slightly open to promote a tiny fade. Then I just ripped it. I knew it would be pretty good the moment it left the clubface, and sure enough, the wind carried the ball a little to the right, just past hole-high. A chip and a putt from there, and I took home the trophy. The most satisfying thing about that shot—the fun thing, really—was pulling it off under pressure.

HOVER THE
CLUBHEAD
AND LIGHTEN
YOUR GRIP.

PLAY THE BALL BACK FOR CRISP CONTACT

H itting the ball solidly, without touching a grain of sand if possible, is the only way to get a lot of distance on this shot. I play the ball farther back in my stance than I would on a shot of similar length from the fairway. Next, I take at least one more club than for a normal shot. When I grip the club, I choke down on the handle for extra control of the club-head. Finally, I make sure I have solid footing—I'm about to make a big swing and I can't afford to slip.

I Stand Tall and Lift My Chin

Just before I start the backswing, I raise my chin well away from my chest. That raises my center of gravity and helps me stand tall throughout the swing, which in turn promotes a solid hit. When I swing, I only apply about 70 percent of my total effort—the extra club I've chosen will produce the distance I need. I swing smoothly into a high finish, keeping my head down until well after the ball is gone.

I TRY TO
PICK THE
BALL
CLEANLY.

THE FULL SWING

❖ ❖ ❖

My swing is a work in
progress and always will be,
starting with sound basics.

❖ 4 ❖
HOW TO SWING

BUILDING AN ACTION TO LAST

After I won the 1997 Masters by 12 strokes with a record score of 270, 18 under par, I wasted no time before celebrating. I do know how to have fun, and I didn't leave anything in the bag. I partied with my buddies, traveled a little and generally had a great time. I knew I would have to come back to earth eventually, but I wasn't in any special hurry to get there.

One night, a week or so later, after the elation had started to die down, I decided to sit down and watch a tape of the entire tournament. I was by myself, so I was really able to concentrate on critiquing my full swing to see if there was some flaw I might be able to work on.

I didn't see one flaw. I saw about 10.

I had struck the ball great that week, but by my standard I felt I had gotten away with murder. My clubshaft was across the line at the top of the backswing and my clubface was closed. My swing plane was too upright. I liked my ball flight, but I was hitting the ball farther with my irons than I should have been because I was delofting the clubface through impact. I didn't like the look of those things, and the more I thought about it, the more I realized I didn't like how my swing felt, either. From a ball-striking standpoint, I was playing better than I knew how.

Even before the tape ended, I committed myself to making some big changes in my swing. Butch had pointed out some of these swing flaws before, and we had been working on them slowly, but I decided right then and there to pick up the pace. I got on the phone and called Butch and let him know what I was thinking. He was all for the swing overhaul I had in mind.

That overhaul took more than a year before the changes really started to kick in. First, my full swing started to look better. Then, the ball started to behave better. Finally, my swing started to feel right, and that's when I knew I had it. I had a very good year in 1999, and in 2000 I played by far the best golf of my life.

The point to this story is, the golf swing will always be a work in progress regardless of how good you are. The goal is to have a swing that is mechanically sound, repeatable, works with every club in your set and holds up under pressure. I don't know if anyone will ever achieve a state of perfection—I know I haven't. But you can bet I'll keep trying.

ONE GRIP FOR ALL SHOTS

· · · · · · · · · · · · · · · · · ·

The grip is the cornerstone of the swing. It is related to almost every element of the swing itself, including path, clubface position, ball position and posture. It isn't really necessary to explain how the grip relates to these other factors, except to say that to have a chance of building a good swing, you need a good grip.

My own grip has evolved over the years. When I was a junior golfer, I preferred a strong left-hand grip, my hand rotated well to my right on the handle of the club. That made both hands much more active during the swing, made it easier to square the clubface at impact, and gave me extra distance. Later, after I grew and became stronger, I weakened my left hand considerably. Today it's in a fairly neutral position, with $2\frac{1}{2}$ knuckles of my left hand showing at address. That's the best position of all in my opinion, and one I know will suit most every golfer.

Whenever I made a grip change, I made sure I had a club in my hands constantly so I could "practice" my new grip. I wanted my new grip to start feeling natural as quickly as possible.

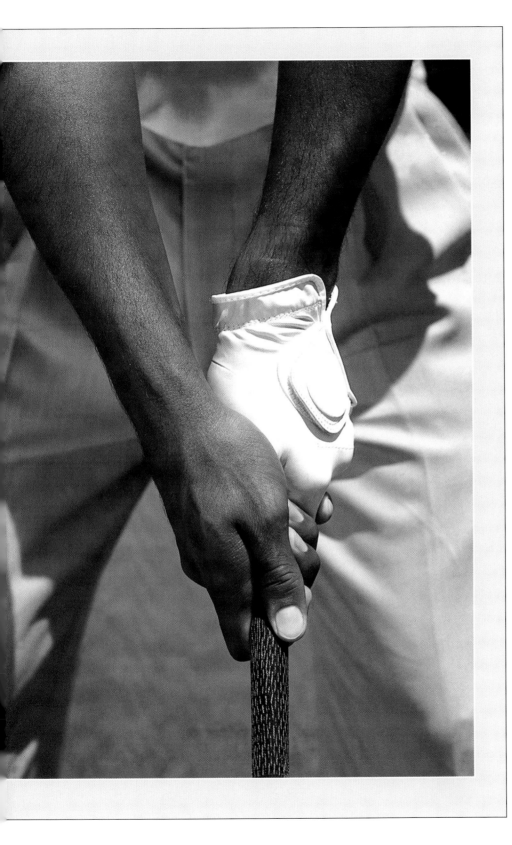

In choosing a particular player to model your swing after, take into consideration the player's height and build. If you're tall and thin, you don't want to copy the swing of a player who is short and stocky.

MY LEFT HAND IS MY CONTROL HAND

· · · · · · · · · · · · · · · ·

The handle of the club runs diagonally across the base of my fingers, from the base of the fore-finger to a point atop the callus pad below my little finger. That provides the best combination of sensitivity and control. At all costs, I avoid placing the handle too far toward the palm of my open left hand. I'll lose clubhead speed and the sensitivity I refer to.

When the left-hand grip is complete and I lower the club into the address position, my thumb should be positioned to the right of center on the handle, and the "V" formed by my right thumb and forefinger should point just outside my right ear.

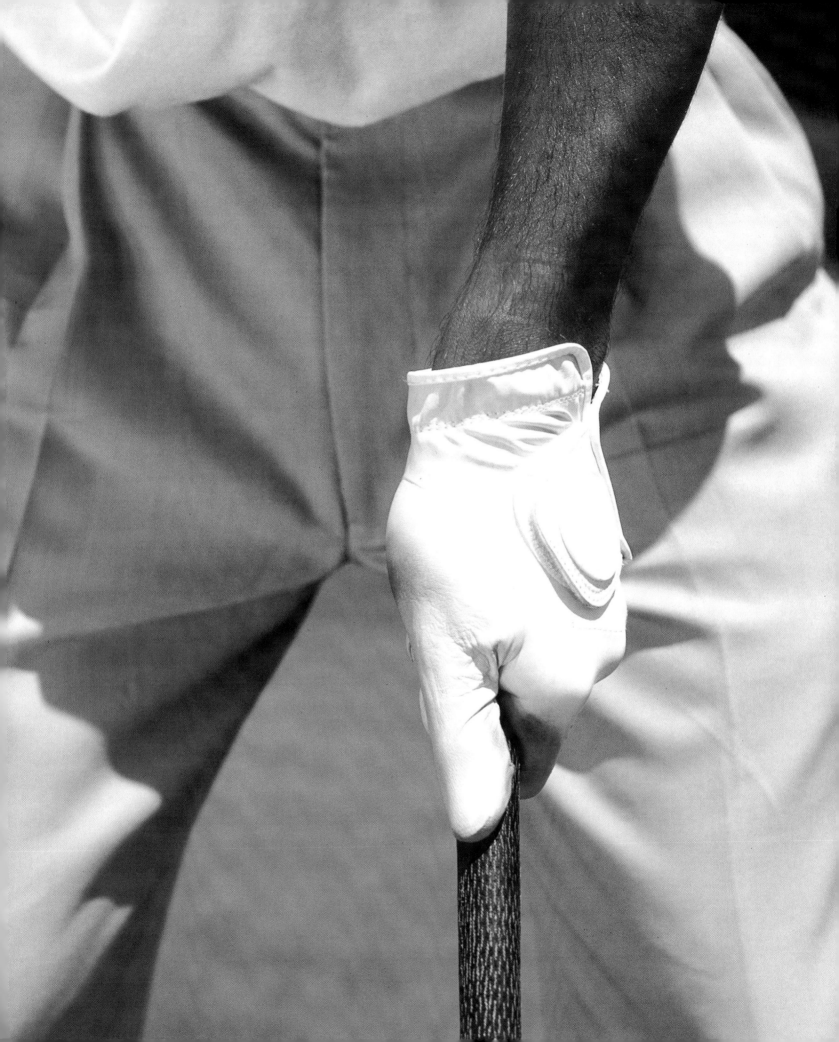

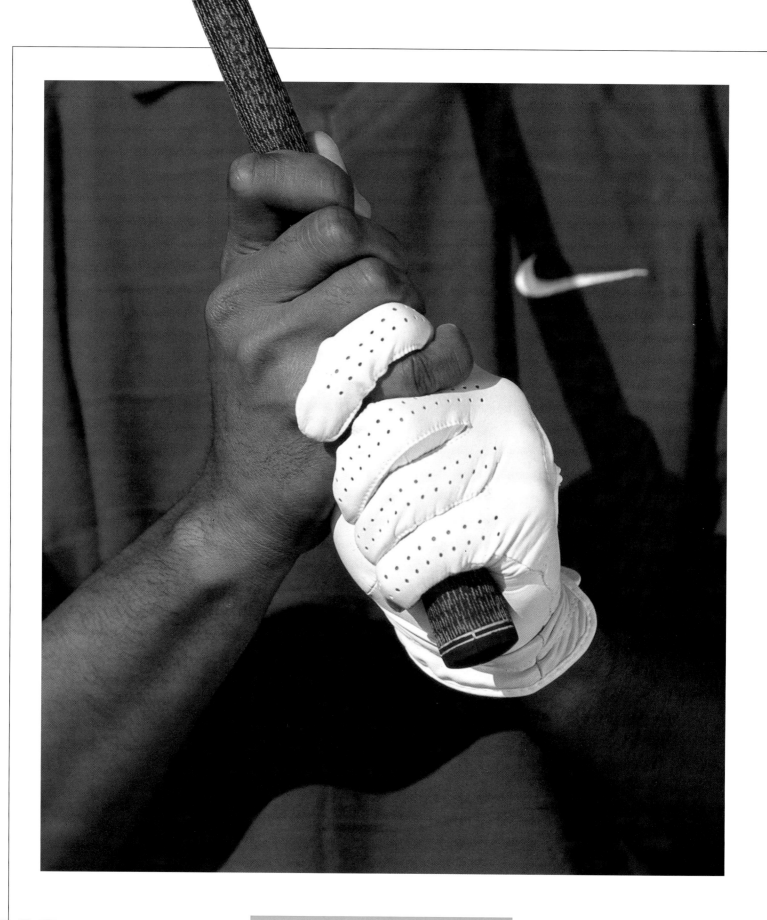

MY RIGHT HAND IS MY SPEED HAND

The right-hand grip is similar to that of the left hand. The main difference is the club is placed more along the fingers. The handle should run from the middle portion of your right index finger to the base of your pinkie. This activates your right hand so it can supply speed on the downswing.

Why I Interlock: As a little boy, I was taught the interlocking grip, the little finger of my right hand laced between the forefinger and middle finger of my left hand. That's how Jack Nicklaus, my idol, did it, and I copied him. It gives me the feeling that my hands can't separate during the swing. I'm in the minority though. Most players prefer the overlapping grip, with the little finger of the right hand placed riding in the notch formed by the left forefinger and middle finger. My feeling is, either way is really just fine.

Never judge your practice sessions on how long you practiced or how many balls you hit. Some of my most productive practice sessions have lasted all of 20 minutes.

PRACTICE RANGE

THE FINISHED PRODUCT

My complete grip provides a sense of snugness and unity between the two hands. They should feel as if they are melded together, almost as if you were born to hold a club. If you don't have that sensation, practice gripping and regripping the club. Keep a club handy just for this purpose.

You should hold the club lightly enough to allow plenty of wrist freedom and to have some feel, but firmly enough to maintain control of the club throughout the swing. The most important thing is to keep your grip pressure steady. If you increase your grip pressure at any point during the swing, it will cost you clubhead speed and control of the club.

On the subject of grip pressure, I believe a lot of amateurs hold the club too tightly because their hands aren't on the club correctly to begin with. To prevent the club from sliding around the fingers and palm, they instinctively tighten their hold, usually at the beginning of the downswing. It proves once again why a technically perfect grip is so important. If your grip is sound, you don't have to think about your hands at all during the swing. You're free to concentrate on the other aspects of good ball striking.

STANCE IS FOR BALANCE—AND POWER

The full swing involves a lot of motion in your upper body. You need a solid foundation to support that motion without stifling it, and that's where stance width comes in.

My Feet Are Too Narrow

This stance width, with my feet about shoulder-width apart, is fine for the short and middle irons. For the driver and fairway woods, however, it's too narrow. There's no way I could maintain my balance and stability with my feet this close together. To do it, I would have to swing at half speed.

My Feet Are Too Wide

Here I have plenty of stability—you'd have a hard time knocking me over if you tried. But remember, the wider your stance, the more you restrict the turning of your hips and shoulders on the back and forward swings.

The Proper Stance Width
Here's a nice blend. For this driver shot, the insides of my feet line up with the outside points of my shoulders. From here I can swing all out with plenty of support from my feet and legs, while at the same time maintaining my ability to turn my hips and shoulders fully.

The right stance width allows me to shift my weight onto my right side while maintaining the flex in my right knee. I'm balanced, fully loaded and ready to go after it on the downswing.

POSTURE: SET UP LIKE AN ATHLETE

Golf is like any other sport that requires movement. You need to be in an athletically ready position so you can respond to movement quickly, smoothly and without losing your balance. The key to good posture is matching up your torso and lower body, so one can react to the other throughout the swing.

Too Much Knee Flex

This is a very common look among amateurs. The extreme amount of knee-bending limits their ability to turn their shoulders fully on the backswing and downswing. The shorter swing arc costs them clubhead speed and accuracy. Another problem is, they flatten the lie of the club. The clubface tends to point to the left, and that, combined with their inability to turn, leads to a pull or slice.

SEE HOW THE CLUB IS SITTING ON ITS HEEL? THAT'S TOO FLAT.

Too Little Knee Flex

If I lock my knees at address, I'm forced to bend excessively at the waist just to reach the ball, a recipe for poor balance throughout the swing. I'll also utilize only 70 percent of my potential power, because my lower body can't contribute to the swing at all. I'm forced to perform the entire motion with my upper body alone, and I can't hit the ball out of my shadow swinging like that.

I MIGHT AS WELL BE STANDING IN A BLOCK OF CEMENT, BECAUSE MY LEGS CAN'T MOVE AT ALL.

Perfect Knee Flex

I want just enough bend in my knees to feel balanced and ready for action. I have a sense of being light on my feet. My weight is distributed evenly from heel to toe, and my hips and shoulders are ready to rotate freely with full cooperation from my legs and feet. Good golf is played from the ground up, meaning that my feet, legs and hips initiate the downswing. If my knees are flexed properly, I can activate the lower body well before my shoulders, arms and hands get involved. The correct sequence of motion is critical.

LIKE A SHORTSTOP IN BASEBALL, I CAN MOVE FREELY IN ANY DIRECTION.

DISTANCE FROM THE BALL SHOULD BE PRECISE

This is closely related to posture and knee flex, so let's talk about it here. Standing the correct distance from the ball at address is vital if I am to make a sound swing. If I'm too close or too far away, I'm forced to make all sorts of anatomical adjustments in order to compensate—and I won't compensate very well.

Top Left—I'm Standing Too Close: This forces my knees into that locked position we talked about. What's more, my spine is too upright. My arms don't have room to swing freely, I can't turn my shoulders on the correct plane, and I'm destined to swing the club way too upright going back and coming down. The ball can go anywhere from this position, and you can bet it won't go very far.

Bottom Left—I'm Too Far Away: This is a horrible position. To reach the ball, I have to extend my arms out from my body. I'm bent over too much at the waist and my knees show too much flex. The tendency is to lift the spine on the backswing and then pitch forward on the downswing. The ball is bound to go anywhere but straight.

Opposite Page—I'm "Measured Off" Just Right: The signs that I'm standing the correct distance from the ball are clear. My arms are hanging comfortably, just a shade outside of vertical. My knees are flexed ever so slightly, I'm bent over at the hips comfortably but not too far, and my weight is evenly distributed between my heels and toes. Now I can turn back and through the ball without changing my spine angle or my knee flex. When I swing, my arms, hands and club have a great chance of returning to the position I've established at address.

BALL POSITION CAN
MAKE OR BREAK YOU

Poor ball position is a silent killer. If you don't place the ball precisely in relation to your stance, the ball will be playing you instead of you playing the ball. You'll have to conjure up some type of weird swing movement just to get the club on the ball, and because of that you'll never be consistent.

On the other hand, if your ball position is correct for the type of club you're hitting, you'll be encouraged to make all the right moves during the swing.

Hands Stay Same Distance from Body

Regardless of the club I am using, my hands remain the same distance from my thighs. That's a great reference point. Although the length of the driver demands that the ball be placed farther away from you than for any other club, I make no wild attempt to reach for the ball. Note that my driver is soled squarely to the ground; the same will be true for the other clubs because they become increasingly upright as they grow shorter.

Common Mistakes

Poorer players are prone to the same errors in ball position. They tend to play the ball too far back in the stance with their longer clubs, perhaps because they feel they can't "reach" the ball through impact if it's too far forward. The result is that they can't turn behind the ball fully on the backswing. With the driver, they are prone to pop-ups, pulls and slices.

With the shorter clubs, the most common mistake is positioning the ball too far forward.

BALL GETS CLOSER WITH SHORTER CLUBS, BUT HANDS STAY SAME DISTANCE FROM BODY.

DRIVER   5-IRON   WEDGE

DRIVER:
TEE FORWARD
TO TURN BEHIND.

NO   YES

BEGINNING THE BACKSWING

Now the real fun is about to begin. Let's start the full swing by setting the club into motion correctly. Notice I said the club, not your body. The reason you've worked hard at positioning your body the right way is so it can transport the club on the proper path and plane throughout the swing.

Start the Club "On Line"
Midway through the backswing, the club should be parallel with your stance line. You get it there by swinging the club back with your shoulders, arms and hands working together smoothly. From here, it's easy to swing the club into perfect position at the top of the backswing.

Don't Let the Club Stray Inside
I've made this mistake many times, and it's a killer. If the club moves too far to the inside midway through the backswing, the shaft aiming to the right of my target, I'm forced to make compensations (I call them "makeup moves") to get the club back on the right track. If I return the club to this position on the down-swing, I'll probably push the ball to the right.

SIX KEYS TO A GREAT BACKSWING

H ere are six checkpoints to ensure you've arrived at a great position at the top of the swing.

■ I let my right elbow come away from my side, but I make sure it points toward the ground.

■ My left shoulder should be turned under my chin. That's easier to do if I keep my chin held high throughout the swing.

■ I keep my right knee flexed, the same way I had it at address.

■ My clubface should be "square" at the top, meaning it is parallel to my left forearm.

■ My left heel stays flat on the ground, which helps restrict my hip turn, creating more torque.

■ My weight is gathered onto my right heel.

**MY RIGHT ELBOW
POINTS DOWN.**

THE MAGIC TRIANGLE

The longer and wider you make your backswing, the more time you give yourself to accumulate speed and power on the downswing. A big shoulder turn is responsible for part of that, but your arms play a big role, too. One of my key thoughts is "wide at the top." I push my left arm away from my head as far as I can, and my right arm goes right along with it. My two arms and elbows form a triangle that helps keep the clubface square and the club on line.

Avoid the Dreaded "Flying Elbow"
As you stretch your left arm away from your body, make darned sure your right elbow doesn't drift recklessly from your side so it winds up pointing behind you. See how the triangle is pointing to the left? The "flying right elbow" means your backswing is loose and disjointed, your arms totally out of sync with what your body is doing. Your downswing will lack power and consistency.

Don't Be Too "Connected," Either
The other way to ruin your triangle is to pinch your right elbow against your side. It shortens your swing, adds tension and makes it difficult to coordinate your arms and body on the downswing.

ELBOW TOO HIGH.

ELBOW TOO LOW.

PRACTICE MAKES PERMANENT

Most golfers encounter streaks where their swing falls into place and they play very well for a short period of time. On the other hand, they fall into slumps where the swing doesn't feel right and the ball goes everywhere except where they're aiming.

My goal—and it may be unattainable—is to groove my swing to the extent that I play my best golf all the time. There is only one way that's going to happen: Practice and more practice. Long ago, I committed myself to the idea that there are no shortcuts to improvement. The best way to ingrain the correct movements and positions is through repetition.

Some players look at practice as drudgery. I happen to love it. Give me a big pile of balls, a new glove, my clubs and some nice turf, and I'm one happy human. Other golfers may outplay me from time to time, but they'll never outwork me.

IN SEARCH OF THE "SLOT"

· ·

I talked about positioning the club correctly mid-way through the backswing. The reason I stress that so much is because you then have a much better chance of setting it in that elusive position known as the "slot" at the top of the swing. Check your reflection in the mirror or a window to see where your club is, then work on setting it correctly.

I've Found the "Slot"

This is the ideal top-of-backswing position. The shaft is parallel to the target line, just as it was midway through the backswing. If I start the down-swing by shifting my lower body to the left and unturning my hips, the club will drop down and approach the ball on the perfect path and plane.

The Club Is "Laid Off"

If the club points to the left of the target at the top, you are prone to "coming over the top" on the downswing. You'll cut across the ball from out to in and hit a slice or pull.

THE CLUB FEELS HEAVIER THAN IT SHOULD AND OUT OF BALANCE TOO.

The Club Is "Across the Line"

If the club points to the right of the target at the top, you are "across the line" and will likely swing the club down too much from the inside. That means a block to the right or a big hook.

FROM HERE, THE CLUB MUST FOLLOW A COMPLICATED ROUTE TO IMPACT.

LET GRAVITY RULE

The faster you swing the club through impact, the farther the ball goes. That's a simple equation, but obtaining speed and power on the downswing is easier said than done. A problem almost every golfer encounters is rushing the downswing—letting loose with everything you have the moment the backswing is complete. When you do that, however, nothing works in proper sequence. The shoulders outrace the arms, the arms outrace the hands and the hands outrace the club. All that speed is expended too soon and the clubhead is actually losing speed as it strikes the ball, when it should be accelerating.

I like to start the downswing by shifting my weight easily back to my left side, and then letting my arms "fall" downward in front of my chest. I don't want my shoulders unwinding so fast that they get way ahead of my arms. By giving my arms a little head start, they work in concert with my shoulders to create a real package of power coming into the ball. That good timing allows me to hit the ball a mile, and I don't have to try very hard to do it.

TIGER TALE:
TRIAL AND ERROR

· ·

I feel very lucky to play golf in an era where so many technological resources are available to optimize my performance, speed my improvement and widen my understanding of the golf swing. There are many ways to get an edge, and technology is one of them. I'm very open-minded toward any innovation that can potentially make me a better player.

I have a lot of tools at my disposal, and I use them all. High-speed video cameras have made it possible to view my swing from several different angles at once and spot even the tiniest flaw. There is no guesswork involved in my swing now— when I hit a bad shot, my understanding of cause and effect enables me to pinpoint the reason imme-

diately. My clubs are manufactured exactly to my specifications, the lofts, lies, shaft flexes and overall weights optimized with painstaking precision. I play a ball that feels and spins just right. My workout regimen is one designed specifically for golf, with emphasis on strength, flexibility and endurance. I've learned a great deal about nutrition and human physiology in general. My understanding of sport psychology has made me a better golfer emotionally and intellectually.

All this to improve the way I whack a ball with a stick! What really excites me is the prospect of even greater breakthroughs in all of these areas. We can't help but be better golfers for it.

DELIVERING THE BIG PAYOFF

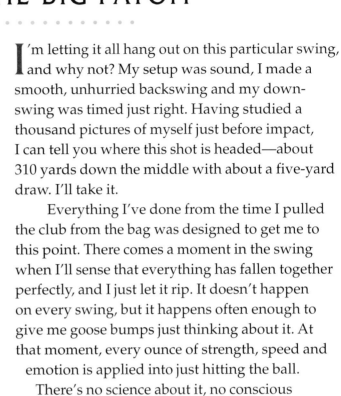

I'm letting it all hang out on this particular swing, and why not? My setup was sound, I made a smooth, unhurried backswing and my downswing was timed just right. Having studied a thousand pictures of myself just before impact, I can tell you where this shot is headed—about 310 yards down the middle with about a five-yard draw. I'll take it.

Everything I've done from the time I pulled the club from the bag was designed to get me to this point. There comes a moment in the swing when I'll sense that everything has fallen together perfectly, and I just let it rip. It doesn't happen on every swing, but it happens often enough to give me goose bumps just thinking about it. At that moment, every ounce of strength, speed and emotion is applied into just hitting the ball. There's no science about it, no conscious thought at all. Just pure joy.

❖5❖
HOW TO FLAG YOUR IRONS

KNOCKING DOWN THE PIN

All things considered, it's easier to play golf during the day than at night. I learned that as a kid when my dad and I used to sneak out on a military golf course near our home and play a few holes just as darkness was gathering. And I learned it all over again at Firestone Country Club in the final round of the 2000 NEC Invitational. I had a substantial lead coming up the 18th hole, and it was so dark people up by the green were holding up cigarette lighters as if it were a rock concert. There had been a three-hour rain delay earlier in the day, and now it was so black I could barely make out the flagstick on the green.

My ball, from what I could see of it, was sitting up pretty well in the first cut of rough. I had 168 yards to the pin. The one thing I didn't want to do was hit an absolutely terrible shot that would lead to a double bogey or something. True, I had a big lead, but I wanted to close things out in style.

I chose an 8-iron and made a couple of practice swings, just to feel where the ground was in relation to the clubhead. I could tell the turf was very firm and felt I'd be able to deliver the ball my normal 8-iron distance. Then I got over the ball, swung and hoped for the best. I saw the ball take off, but then lost it in the darkness about 30 yards into its flight. The next thing I heard was a huge roar from the gallery up by the green. My ball had come to rest two feet from the hole, and the birdie gave me the kind of victory I was looking for.

Looking back, I suppose I could have used a pitching wedge and played the ball just short of the green, to avoid the bunkers and any real trouble. But whenever I get an iron in my hands, my first instinct is to be aggressive. The irons are the true offensive weapons in golf. I always feel a surge of excitement just pulling an iron from the bag, because that's where the process of making birdies really begins. If you're capable of hitting the ball close to the hole, you're capable of shooting low scores.

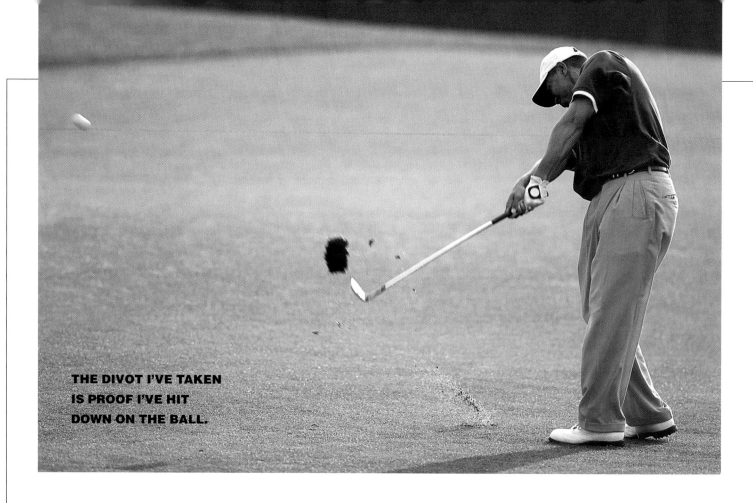

**THE DIVOT I'VE TAKEN
IS PROOF I'VE HIT
DOWN ON THE BALL.**

THE BASIC EQUATION

From a scientific standpoint, golf is a game of opposites. I think that's what makes it such a hard game for some people. A lot of the things that occur when the club strikes the ball are just the opposite of what your instincts tell you should happen. For instance, a shot that slices to the right occurs because the clubhead, square to the target line, is traveling to the left at impact. Another example is grip pressure. If you grip the club tightly in an effort to hit the ball harder, you end up swinging the club even slower, because tight muscles don't move as fast as loose muscles.

The best example falls in the area of iron play. In order to get the ball airborne, you must hit down on it. Countless golfers try to help get the ball in the air by swinging up on the ball. That makes it go down—a topped shot, or a thin one at best.

Hitting down not only gets the ball in the air, it imparts backspin and enables the ball to fly true.

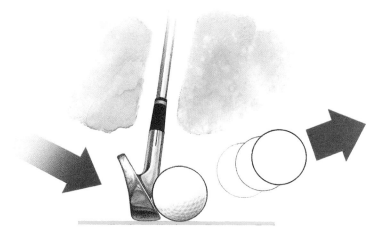

When the clubhead is traveling downward at impact, physics demand that the ball fly upward.

A PRIMER ON BALL POSITION

· · · · · · · · · · · · · · · · ·

The golf club travels in a circular path during the swing, with the lowest point of the circle occurring directly below your sternum. To make the clubhead contact the ball while it's still moving downward (before it reaches the bottom of the circle), you need to position the ball correctly in relation to your body.

The Driver: The ball is placed opposite my left heel. The clubhead will be moving level to slightly upward when it contacts the ball. The driver is the only club you want to hit slightly on the upswing.

The 5-iron: The ball is positioned slightly forward of center at address. Nevertheless, I still can hit down on the ball because my body moves forward laterally on the down-swing, which moves the bottom point of the swing closer to the target.

The Pitching Wedge: I want to hit down a bit more sharply on the ball with my wedges. Therefore, I play the ball dead in the center of my stance. I have less lateral body movement on my short irons because the swing is shorter, so I don't want to position the ball forward of center.

PITCHING WEDGE   5-IRON   DRIVER

BUILDING A STABLE BASE

· · · · · · · · · · · · · · · · · · · ·

On every shot, you need a combination of balance, stability and ease of movement. Those factors are largely determined by stance width—how far apart you position your feet at address. Stance width is especially important with your irons, as they are precision clubs that demand a rock-solid base with your lower body.

▲ *The Driver and Woods from the Fairway:* My feet are spread wide to accommodate my big shoulder turn and fast upper-body movement during the swing. A narrower stance would encourage a sway; a wider stance would limit my weight shift.

Three things happen when I choke down on my irons: I hit the ball a bit straighter, I get a lower ball flight, and the ball doesn't check up as quickly when it hits the green.

CHOKE GASP!

▲ *Short Shots:* My swing with the short irons isn't super long, and I rarely swing with all my effort. Therefore, I don't need a wide base. When I'm pitching or chipping, my stance is narrower still.

◀ *The 5-iron:* As the club becomes shorter, my stance width becomes narrower. My stance is wide enough to allow me to keep my balance, but not so far apart that it restricts motion in my upper body. With each club, it is important to be consistent with my stance width on every shot. That is the only way to produce consistent results.

THERE'S NO STOPPING
THIS BACKSWING.

KEEP YOUR CHIN UP

. . . .

Good posture is important on every shot. At address I make sure my back is fairly straight and that I have a bit of flex in my knees. My body is now prepared to move freely in any direction during the swing.

One of the most important aspects of good posture is to hold your chin high at address. It's something Butch Harmon and I check constantly. You want your chin well off your chest so your left shoulder has plenty of room to turn under your chin on the backswing. This is one of my key thoughts.

The Finished Product

As you can see, my shoulders are turning freely with no interference from my chin. This wasn't always the case. I used to stand too close to the ball, which caused me to lower my chin just to see the ball clearly when I looked down at address. I sometimes felt crowded, and no wonder—there was very little room for my shoulders to turn and my arms to swing. Today I stand farther from the ball, with my head held high throughout the swing. My change in posture allows me to turn freely, back and through.

A 9-iron shot won't hook or slice as much as a 5-iron shot. The more loft you have, the less sidespin you can impart on the ball.

THINK "WIDE" ON THE BACKSWING

The proper backswing is a combination of horizontal and vertical movement. Most amateurs err on the vertical side—they start the swing by lifting the arms straight up and cocking the wrists immediately. Because the backswing is too vertical, the downswing is too vertical as well. The tendency is to chop down on the ball instead of swinging through it smoothly.

Don't forget the "horizontal" part of the backswing. That means establishing a nice, wide swing arc as soon as you move the club back. I have the feeling of stretching my hands and arms away from my body early in the backswing, my wrists beginning to cock naturally after the clubhead reaches about knee height. That helps me accumulate power and also ensures that my downswing won't be too steep.

A Bad Start

The takeaway I'm modeling here is too steep and vertical. The arc of my swing is narrow already, and by the time I get to the top of the swing it will be too late to widen it. You can bet the downswing will be too steep, too. That means deep divots, fat shots and an inconsistent ball flight.

NO
A TIGHT, NARROW, STEEP BACKSWING.

YES

**HOW FAR FROM MY
HEAD CAN I MOVE
MY HANDS?**

I UNIFY MY BACKSWING

I believe in a nice, wide backswing, but I don't like a backswing that is too loose. I don't want my arms running away from my upper body. That would lead to a "fake backswing"—the club reaching parallel, but only due to excessive wrist-cocking or the arms swinging back too far. That leads to a weak downswing in which you slap at the ball with your hands and arms alone.

I try to swing the club back with everything—hips, shoulders, arms and hands—working together. When I turn my shoulders fully, they accommodate the swinging of my arms to create a strong, unified package at the top of the backswing.

Tighten That Turn
One way to prevent your arms from out-racing your upper body is to check the position of your right arm at various stages of the backswing. When Butch and I work together, he checks that my right arm is kept fairly close to my side and in front of my torso as I complete my shoulder turn. I don't like my arms to feel cramped, but I don't want them straying too far from my body, either.

MY SHOULDERS AND
ARMS TRANSPORT THE
CLUB TOGETHER.

START DOWN SLOW

. . . .

When good players talk about "getting too quick," they're almost always talking about the first move down from the top of the back-swing. The beginning of the downswing can't be rushed. You want your swing to gather speed gradually, so that everything works in sequence and the clubhead reaches its maximum speed at impact. If you start down suddenly, all your speed and power are gone by the time you reach impact. Your timing and mechanics are shot, too.

Remember, there can only be one fast moment in the swing, and it had better be when the club strikes the ball.

SLOW TO HERE, THEN POUR ON THE POWER.

DOWN AND THROUGH

· ·

One of the keys to good ball striking is to hit *through* the ball, not at it. In my mind, the ball is merely an object that is in the way of the clubhead as it tears through the hitting area. I don't try to end my swing abruptly after the ball is struck. I try to keep the clubhead accelerating down the target line as long as I comfortably can.

TIGER TALE:
A VERY ACCEPTABLE MISS

My swing tendencies change a bit from day to day. That's part of golf; for no discernible reason your misses might one day be pulls to the left, the next day fades a bit too far to the right. These small shifts in ball flight aren't necessarily disastrous, provided you allow for them.

I learned this lesson at the 1997 Mercedes Championship, where I found myself tied with Tom Lehman after 54 holes. Heavy rain canceled the last round just after play got under way, so it all came down to a sudden-death playoff between Tom and me.

The playoff began at the 186-yard, par-3 seventh hole, in a light rain. It was also cold. Tom drew the honor, and darned if he didn't hit his ball in the water to the left of the green. Knowing I needed only a par to win, I didn't want to flirt with the left side of the green, where the pin was located dangerously close to the water Tom had just visited. I aimed well to the right, taking a key factor into consideration: My misses on the range during my warm-up tended to be to the left. The way I figured it, if I hit the ball exactly where I was aiming, I could take two putts and still win. If I happened to hook the ball a bit, so much the better.

I hit a 6-iron and sure enough, the ball drew to the left more than I anticipated. I was sure glad I aimed well to the right, because the ball landed eight inches from the hole and stopped dead. I tapped in for birdie and came away with a trophy and a lesson in course management I carry with me to this day.

A TALE OF TWO DIVOTS

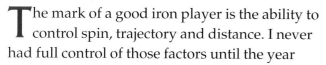

The mark of a good iron player is the ability to control spin, trajectory and distance. I never had full control of those factors until the year following my victory in the 1997 Masters. Only after a long period of hard work was I able to get my iron play where I wanted it. One of the swing changes I made altered the look of my divots, especially with my short and middle irons. Prior to 1997, I took deep, heavy divots that sometimes were as big as dinner plates. The divots may have looked cool flying through the air, but they showed my downswing was too steep and that I was delofting the clubface through impact. As a result I couldn't adjust the ball's spin, trajectory or distance worth a darn. The swing change I made shallowed out my swing so the clubhead approached the ball at an angle that was closer to level.

The divots I took after the swing change looked a lot different. Instead of being long and deep, they were long and shallow, about the size of a dollar bill. I can still take a big divot when I have to, but the standard divot should be long and thin.

THIS IS THE LOOK OF A PERFECT DIVOT.

THIS DIVOT
IS TOO BIG!

More Causes of Deep Divots

There are other reasons why divots can be deep and irregular. It may be that your ball is positioned too far back in your stance, which necessitates a steep angle of approach with the clubhead. You may be throwing the clubhead at the ball with your arms and hands alone, instead of assisting with your shoulders. Or you may be "coming over the top" on the downswing, in which case the gash made by your divot points well to the left of your target line.

A SWEET FINISH

The look of my follow-through serves as sort of a road map for what happened earlier in my swing. See how my arms are extended? That shows my swing was real wide, with good extension through the ball. See how far my shoulders have unwound? That shows my swing was predicated on a full shoulder turn instead of just my hands and arms. Finally, see how the toe of the club points straight down? That proves I didn't rotate the club excessively with my hands through impact. For it to arrive at this position, I had to release the club naturally.

THE FEELING HERE IS ONE OF THROWING THE CLUBHEAD DOWN THE LINE WITH MY RIGHT HAND.

"CHASE" THE BALL WITH YOUR RIGHT HAND

O n second shots into long par 4s and short par 5s, you're aiming at a pretty small target. Accuracy is extremely important and not all that easy to achieve. Keep in mind, the fairway wood is a lot longer than, say, your 7-iron and thus is harder to control. The best key for keeping the ball on the straight and narrow is to make the clubhead track straight down the target line for as long as possible after impact. You should feel you are chasing the ball into the distance with your right hand, keeping the clubhead low to the ground and allowing your right arm to extend fully after it has struck the ball. This will keep the clubface square to the target for a longer period through impact.

WHEN I MUST TURN THE BALL LEFT

Only after years of practice am I able to shape my tee shots at will without changing the basic character of my swing. The benefit of all this work led to my winning my sixth professional major, and the fourth in a row, the 2001 Masters. The 13th hole at Augusta National is a par 5 that bends sharply to the left about 230 yards out from the tee. The player who can hit a long, controlled draw on demand has a big advantage there, for once the ball turns the corner, it can scamper to within 200 yards of the green. And because of the elusive nature of the firm, undulating green, it's a treat to have a middle iron in your hand to use on your approach shot.

Long before I arrived at Augusta for the 2001 Masters, I practiced that draw with my driver and 3-wood. For two months solid, I would devote a little extra time on the practice tee with that specific shot in my mind's eye. I don't consciously change my mechanics. I do it by feel. My last thought before I take the club back is "Draw." I got good at hitting the shot in practice, but would it hold up under pressure?

I found out in the final round. Nursing a narrow lead over Phil Mickelson and David Duval, I stood on the 13th tee determined to bring off that hard, piercing draw. Filled with the confidence that comes from knowing you've prepared yourself well, I grabbed my 3-wood and just ripped the tee shot. The ball not only turned the corner, it didn't stop rolling until it came to rest in a perfect lie, 183 yards from the green. I hit the green easily, and the tap-in birdie that followed kept my lead intact—a lead, as it turned out, I wouldn't lose.

❖7❖
HOW TO SMOKE THE DRIVER

GOING WITH ALL YOU'VE GOT

If one club in my bag qualifies as being more important than any other, it's the driver. A lot of people will tell you it's the putter simply because more strokes are made with the flat stick during a round than with any other club. But the driver gets my vote for several reasons. A good drive makes all things possible. My chances of making a birdie or eagle are increased enormously when I crush the ball long and straight. What's more, if my swing with the driver is sound, my swing with the irons tends to be good as well. As the driver goes, so goes the rest of my game from tee to green.

But the biggest thing about the driver isn't tactical or mechanical. To me, the driver has the special capability of giving me an emotional lift and a big edge psychologically. A super drive that stops on the center mowing stripe fills me with strength, energy and confidence.

Nowhere was the emotional lift from a good drive more apparent—or more necessary—than on the final hole of the 2001 Masters. I came to the 18th tee knowing I had the tournament sewn up—provided I made a par 4. A bogey would put me in a playoff against David Duval. This was not a time to play defensively. I chose the driver and committed myself to ripping the ball almost as hard as I could. I set up to play a fade, and swung as aggressively as I had all week.

Television viewers saw me hold my finish extra long, and they might have thought I was just enjoying the moment, but I was trying to watch my ball finish. It literally went out of my sight. I thought I might have faded the ball too much around the corner of the dogleg, that it could have drifted into the trees on the right. As I walked up the fairway, I saw a ball sitting in the right rough, but it was Phil Mickelson's, not mine. I looked farther up ahead, and lo and behold, there was my ball, sitting pretty in the fairway, only 78 yards from the green. Man, was I relieved—and excited. The little wedge shot I had left was nothing, and one putt later, I had my second green jacket and fourth straight major championship.

A FOUNDATION FOR POWER

My stance is wider with the driver than for any other club. That's because my driver swing is longer, wider and (on the downswing at least) a lot faster. Spreading my feet slightly wider than my shoulders gives me the stability I need to really go after it. I flex my knees just a little, enough to make them feel alive and promote easy movement in my trunk and torso.

I also pay close attention to my foot position at address. I've found that by flaring my right foot out to my right ever so slightly, I'm able to make a modest hip turn without straining my knee and thigh. As for my left foot, I flare it out slightly in the opposite direction, toward the target. This prevents me from turning my hips too far on the backswing, and allows me to rotate my upper body freely on the downswing and into my follow-through without putting too much pressure on my leg and back.

Finally, I like to angle my knee inward just a bit at address. That encourages me to turn rather than slide on the backswing, and makes it easier to shift my weight to the left on the downswing.

Extra Width for Extra Distance
When I'm playing a par 5 that is reachable in two and the fairway is fairly wide, I sometimes will swing as hard as I can. When I plan to go all out with the driver, I spread my feet even wider than normal. That gives me a firmer base so I won't lose my balance. What's more, a wider stance helps me station most of my weight on my right side. One of the keys to distance is keeping the upper body to the right of the ball on the downswing, and a wider stance helps me do that. The wider the stance, the more difficult it is to sway laterally on the forward swing.

A WELL-BUILT HOUSE IS WIDEST AT THE FOUNDATION. THE SAME GOES FOR MY SETUP— MY FEET ARE WIDER THAN MY SHOULDERS.

WIDER

A POWERFUL START

. . . .

The sequence of motion on the backswing is the same for the driver as for every other club. But I do pay special attention to my hips. I make absolutely sure that my hips turn rather than slide to my right. Turning the hips is one of the first signs I'm accumulating power. This rotary motion in my hips and shoulders is much like loading a giant spring. By the time I reach the top, my hips and shoulders are primed to unload with tremendous speed.

HIPS SLIDE— A KILLER FAULT.

HIPS TURN NICELY.

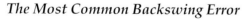

The Most Common Backswing Error
Shifting your hips laterally to the right just kills your backswing. If your right hip moves outside of your right foot, you have to slide back to the left just to hit the ball. It's hard to time that move properly. What's more, you've cut your power by about 50 percent, because a sliding motion on the

downswing isn't anywhere near as powerful as a rotary unwinding of the hips and shoulders. A good thought is to keep your weight on the inside portion of your right foot, keeping the angle of your right leg constant throughout the backswing. This is something I've worked on since I was a kid; it is an absolute trademark of my swing.

THE SWING THAT
WON THE SLAM

. . . .

When I began working with Butch Harmon in 1993, my swing was pretty rough around the edges. At age 17 I had some knowledge of swing mechanics, but certainly not enough to understand fully what I had to improve upon, and how to go about improving it.

The swings you see here, photographed in 2000, result from many years of study, analysis and practice. In some ways, there isn't much room for improvement, but therein lies the catch: It's the little modifications you make at the end that are the hardest to incorporate into your game. Sometimes the changes are so subtle they are barely visible to the naked eye and very difficult to implement, feel-wise, into the swing.

But I'm pleased with my progress. Butch and I set out to improve the way my body functioned during the swing, with the intent of making the *club* perform in the most efficient way possible. Our goal was to design a swing that was powerful, efficient, accurate, repeatable and would work with every club in the bag.

What can you learn from the swing you see here? If I were drawing up a short list of things to copy, it would include:

■ I turn my shoulders as far as possible without letting the range of motion disrupt my spine angle or the position of my right leg.

■ I make my shoulders and arms work together throughout the swing. I don't let one get too far ahead of or behind the other. That's one of the secrets of good rhythm and tempo.

■ I keep the clubface square throughout the swing. That means, the clubface is parallel with the left wrist and forearm.

■ I strive to get the sequence of motion on the downswing just right. My lower body leads the way, followed by my shoulders, arms and hands.

■ I hit through the ball, not at it. I want to keep the clubhead traveling fairly low to the ground for a brief period after impact. That thought will promote solid contact, accuracy and maximum distance.

I START MY SWING SLOWLY AND SMOOTHLY, SETTING THE STAGE FOR WHAT YOU SEE ON THE FOLLOWING PAGES.

WHEN ALL GOES RIGHT,
I ARRIVE AT THE FINISH
YOU SEE HERE.

THINK "LONG AND WIDE"

I have two goals on my takeaway: To establish a very wide swing arc, and to shift my weight fully to my right side without sliding to my right. I try to extend the butt end of the shaft as far from my right hip as I possibly can, my shoulders turning to make it possible. You'll notice that my right leg is angled toward the target a bit even though I've clearly shifted my weight onto my right side.

MY SHOULDERS TURN FARTHER THAN MY HIPS

· ·

With the driver, I turn my shoulders as far as they'll go. My hips turn, too, but my shoulders turn a lot farther. There should be a healthy feeling of tension and resistance down your left side at the top. From here, all I have to do is unwind my hips a bit, and my shoulders will follow, unturning with tremendous speed on the downswing.

When I'm driving downwind I often leave the driver in the bag and go with my 3-wood. I carry the ball just as far, and increase my chances of hitting the ball straight.

I TURN MY LEFT SHOULDER UNDER MY CHIN

· · · · · · · · · · · · · · · ·

I know I'm making a full shoulder turn when my left shoulder turns under my chin. I try to turn my shoulders at least 90 degrees from their position at address, enough so my left shoulder is well behind the ball at the top. Butch Harmon tells me that Ben Hogan used to wear out his shirts at the point where the left shoulder moved under the chin.

A full shoulder turn means I don't have to force the issue on the downswing. My shoulders will unwind fast but smoothly, carrying the arms along with them on their powerful route to impact.

TIGER TALE: DRIVING WITH DISTRACTION

The driver swing is the most physical act in all of golf. But there's a strong mental aspect to it, too. To consistently drive the ball long and straight, you need to be single-minded about what you're doing. You must be totally impervious to distractions and immune to thoughts that can make your swing fall to pieces. Because the driver swing is long and a bit violent in terms of the sheer speed you're trying to generate, timing is extremely important. If you allow something to break your concentration and upset your rhythm or tempo, you're in deep trouble.

Staying focused can be a tall order for me, simply because there are large numbers of people very close by on virtually every drive I hit.

The gallery grows so quiet when I'm preparing to hit that when someone does speak or a camera clicks, it can sound like a bomb going off. My goal is to be so focused that I don't hear these disruptions—or at least don't allow them to influence my swing.

In the final round of the 2001 Masters, I arrived at the 15th tee doing my best to protect a fragile one-stroke lead over David Duval. The drive on the 15th, a reachable par 5, is critical. A long, accurate tee shot sets up a middle-iron approach over water to a firm, sloping green. You really need a birdie there to avoid giving a shot back to the field. This was on my mind as I conducted my preshot routine then set up over the ball.

I made a nice, full backswing and made my first move down from the top, the club dropping right into the "slot." Then, out of nowhere, a camera clicked. Startled badly, I somehow managed to stop my downswing before the club hit the ball. And I'm glad I did, or I might not have gotten that second green jacket.

It goes to show that good driving is partly the result of having good concentration and presence of mind. I was focused on what I was doing that day, yet somehow aware of my surroundings. If I can manage myself with a couple of hundred people within whispering distance, you can learn to do it on Saturday mornings with only a couple of buddies nearby.

IT'S COOL TO BE SQUARE

The position you establish at the top serves as a preview of where you'll be at impact. One of my goals is to achieve a "square" clubface at the top of the backswing, meaning it should be parallel with my left forearm. If the toe of the clubhead were pointing more toward the ground, my clubface would be open and I'd tend to hit a big slice. If the club-face were aimed dead at the sky, the clubface would be closed and I'd lean toward hitting a big hook.

KEEP CLUB SHORT OF PARALLEL

· ·

I believe in a big shoulder turn, but I don't like the club dipping past parallel with the ground. Actually, the shoulders aren't to blame for the club going back too far. It happens because the left arm bends too much at the elbow or the hands don't maintain a firm hold on the club. When the shaft extends beyond parallel, you tend to "throw" the club from the top with the hands, rather than letting the unturning of the shoulders transport the club into a sound position on the downswing.

LOWER BODY LEADS THE WAY

On the downswing, the sequence of motion is from the ground up. First you shift your weight to your left leg, then you turn your hips with all you've got. The shoulders come next; as you can see in the photo, my shoulders are still square to the target even though my hips are aligned well to the left. The arms and hands come last. If you've performed everything in order, they'll deliver the clubhead into the ball along the correct inside path.

Remember, the chain of events occurs slowly at first. If you rush, you'll likely unwind your shoulders too soon and perform the dreaded "over the top" move, where the club is delivered into the ball on an out-to-in path. That means a loss of power and, more than likely, a big slice to the right.

FOR MORE YARDS, I "SNAP" MY LEFT LEG

When I need an extra 20 yards, I incorporate a special move in my lower body just before impact. I've found that by snapping my left leg straight, my hips clear faster and speed up the movement of my shoulders, arms and legs. This is an unorthodox move meant solely for power. Byron Nelson and many other great ball strikers concentrate on maintaining a bit of flex in their left leg through impact, as that tends to keep the clubhead moving along the target line longer. But for extra distance, I straighten that left leg as quickly as I can on the through-swing.

When you absolutely have to hit the ball straight, try teeing the ball a little lower. It won't curve as much to the left or right.

MY SHOULDERS AND ARMS MATCH UP

· ·

One swing problem I have to monitor constantly is not letting my arms lag too far behind my upper body on the downswing. Because my hips and shoulders unwind so quickly, they sometimes outrace my arms. The result is that I drag the clubhead into the ball from far inside the target line, forcing me to rotate my hands furiously to square the clubface at impact. If I don't rotate the hands enough I push the ball to the right; if I rotate them too much I hit a big hook. This makes for an inconsistent ball flight.

My goal, as you can see in this photo taken just after impact, is to keep my arms in front of my body as much as possible throughout the downswing. Notice that my arms are in front of my chest, my shoulders aligned only slightly left of the target line. I've timed everything very well on this swing, and you can bet the ball flew a mile in a controlled direction.